Copyright©PeterA.Fitzgerald

ALLEN SMITHEE ACADEMY

A FILM SCREENPLAY
by
P.A. FITZGERALD

PRIVATE AND CONFIDENTIAL
This original Film Screenplay& TV Pilot remains
the Property of Peter A. Fitzgerald, the
sole creator and writer. Mobile (+61) 478174032
P.O Box246 MORISETT N.S.W. 2264
Australia. Website: whalesroad.com
And equal share property of
Helen. M. Fitzgerald and Jane Fitzgerald
and C. Pasvolsky all contactable 0478174032.
Based on P.A. Fitzgerald's
treatments, short stories & Screenplay Reg AWG &
National Library of Australia.
Illustration by Jay Lee.
Typesetting by Rack and Rune Publishing.

ISBN: 978-1-7635739-3-2
Copyright © P.A Fitzgerald

THE ALLEN SMITHEE ACADEMY
A FILM SCREENPLAY
by
P.A. FITZGERALD

THUMBNAIL SUMMARY:

A diverse group of ambitious and quirky young-twenties STEVEN SPIELBERG, KATHRYN BIGELOW and COEN Brothers WANNABES, head to a flash new Private University's ACADEMY OF FILM, TELEVISION and ACTING in MELBOURNE to acquire the requisite skills to make their marks in the Film, Theatre and TV Entertainment Industries.

"BLOCKBUSTER CHRONICLES" is a unique place: it's where Reality, Drama, Comedy, myriad Creative Ideas, Dreams and Magic Realism, blur, intersect, confront and collide: just as they do in Film and Television, as well as on the World Stage of human life. But the world of these Film Students and their Teachers is an ever-changing place where a multitude of original stories are told, and where almost anything that can happen most assuredly will.

Copyright(c) Peter Anthony Fitzgerald

THE ALLEN SMITHEE ACADEMY
by
Peter Anthony Fitzgerald

EXT. ROOF TOP HIGH RISE BUILDING. LATE AFTERNOON 1

SLOW PAN ACROSS MELBOURNE SKYLINE AND DISTANT BEACH.

VOICES OFF Suddenly there's swearing and yelling as a casually dressed athletic man in his late 30's (BILLY O'LEARY) sprints across the roof-top pursued by a furious-black-suited bald man of 50 waving a gun in the air. BILLY races along the edge of the building glancing over the side for an escape route. His pursuer is close and ready to shoot.
WIDE: The POV expands to panoramic shot: a Film Crew shoots this from across the roof top. An academic looking WOMAN ANNETTE KRIEL(50) looks academic in serious glasses, white blouse and designer Jeans. She approaches them shouting at "everyone"..

ANNETTE (TO DOP AND CREW)
Cut! Okay take five, everybody.

Both running ACTORS stop instantly as she walks briskly towards them.

ANNETTE
We've almost got it BILLY. We'll go again in 5, from the start. And you need more anger RAY…no, make that Rage! This time, shoot twice: the second shot will hit him in the shoulder. BILLY…clutch your upper back as if the bullet hurls you almost over the edge. So RAY.s, elated with the shot and curses BILLY You pause on the ledge for a few seconds before your fall to the safety-net: and fall like you're already unconscious, Okay?

Her raised eyebrows question both ACTORS "are on the same page".

BILLY (HALF JOKING)

You know I'm an aspiring actor ANNETTE. So what's my motivation for this scene?

ANNETTE (WRY GRIN)

Well you have several motivations I suppose: firstly, try not to die doing the stunt; secondly, it will pay you six grand instead of your usual daily rate of $1000; and thirdly, if you don't, you'll be THROWN off the roof by the me and the crew.

BILLY

Got it! Motivation's over-rated anyway.

Two minutes later the chase re starts and BILLY again shows his excellent physical skills, dropping seventy metres to the soft landing mats, which the second DOP films from below. The crew high five him as he walks to the catering area and accepts a can of Coca Cola. ECU ANNETTE'S face is suddenly seen leaning over the top and nodding at the 2ND D.O.P who gives her his two thumbs up to say it's good.

ANNETTE

Okay, that's a wrap everyone. Let's call it a day.

Her head disappears from above and they all start winding up. There's a sudden whizzing sound and then a flash of something shiny. BILLY and the remaining crew suddenly look up and cry out just as a small Metallic-object comes hurtling towards them and strikes BILLY's head. He removes it from his now bloody scalp and stares at it.

BILLY

It's…it's fricking Russian Space junk! Motherfu…

He suddenly turns white as a sheet, clutches his forehead and drops dead. The crew members try to revive him but everything in the frame slows visually and urgent voices too become slow and distorted.
CLOSE on BILLY shows a trickle of blood running down his face. But he's at peace. The POV now slowly spirals up towards fading clouds as dusk falls to the aural accompaniment of a distorted ambulance's siren.

2 INT. EDWARD KELLY 111 UNIVERSITY FUNCTIONS HALL LATE MORNING

The first signs of people preparing for a significant occasion at the brand-new EDWARD KELLY 111 Academy of Film, Television, Theatre and KINETIC Acting (EKAFTTWA) located in inner Melbourne: CLEANERS are hard at it, TECHNICIANS set up the Sound and TV Systems and OTHERS affix sizable female and male portrait photos to display on the stage. Two young WOMEN set up floral displays. Busy CATERERS hurry to and fro. It's a grand operation

3 INT. FLEMINGTON RACETRACK AND PUNTERS BAR. LATE MORNING

PERCY (PERCE) SLATER (64, solid, excessive product in his died black hair) and EDDY, AKA SWIFTY, KELLY 111 (70, paunchy, filthy rich) in expensive casual attire, lay big bets for a horse race, and drink beers.

PERCY (LOOKING AT GOLD HIS WATCH)

Better take it a bit easy with the sauce EDDY. Only another 9 hours till your big speech and shindig.

KELLY looks slightly under the weather already.

> ### EDWARD (EDDY) KELLY 111
> Piece of cake PERCY Plenty of time for an hour-long kip after the third race.

4 EXT. PICTURESQUE OLD CHURCHYARD. MELBOURNE. MIDDAY

MIKE O'LEARY (personable, glasses, 55) looks at the end of his tether. He sits alone among gravestones in the grounds of a church graveyard.
He wears a dark suit and sips frequently from a hip flask.
CU: A Funeral Service leaflet he examines. It's for BILLY O'LEARY. It features five portrait photos on the first page: they feature their deceased parents, BILLY, and wife CARLY, their 17-year-old twins JOSH and SARAH, as well as MIKE, BILLY'S ELDER BROTHER. Under the photos is the order of Service and some song lyrics.
MIKE sorts through notes with the heading "Eulogy."
MIKE sips from a silver flask as rain starts to fall, oblivious to his brother BILLY'S GHOST, which has just materialized and now sits on a gravestone nearby looking "pissed off". MIKE unzips the collar of his coat and a sleepy bulldog puppy peeps out. MIKE stands unsteadily and checks the time on the service pages against his watch.

> ### MICK (TO THE PUP)
> Shite! Sheiser! Merde! Let's went, BIFF.

BIFF instantly falls asleep. MIKE runs to a VESPA Scooter and rides towards a main road. DISSOLVE TO:

5 EXT.CREMATORIUM CARPARK.MORNING 5

MIKE's soaked as he pulls up in the CREMATORIUM's woodland-fringed carpark. He stares at three adjoining chapels, all seemingly full of MOURNERS and all seemingly identical. The PUP snores on. CUT TO

6 EXT/INT CREMATORIUM & EKAFTTA PREP

A SERIES OF JUMP CUTS tO AND FROM THE FUNERAL to Preparations for the ACADEMY'S Opening NIGHT.

7 EXT.CREMATORIUM PARK.MORNING

The Rain's set in. MIKE's under a tree practising his Eulogy but he's drunk, and drops his glasses in a muddy puddle. Near the Chapels, he can't get all the mud off his glasses' lenses. His vision's clearly terrible without them.

8 INT. CREMATORIUM. CHAPEL 1. LATE MORNING

He enters Chapel 1 and sees a dozen seated people who give him strange looks. He strides past them towards the dais and microphone. He peers at the glass-covered casket for a second and salutes it, but panics when he still can't see properly. Resignedly he pockets his notes and begins, despite at first being unable to make out any faces among the mourners.

MIKE

I realize it's short-sighted of me

He rubs his glasses lens again

> but I can't see the bloody eulogy. Let me start by saying that 39 is too damn young for someone so full of life to drop off the perch. But my brother BILLY loved fast times, fast motor bikes and fast cars, and according to his "hilarious when drunk" wife CARLY – he loved fast sex, as well, after a

MIKE(CONT.)

few drinks…Sorry… Inappropriate! (Muttering to himself) and he drank Tequilas the way you and I drink…uh..

He gets some mud off one lens with spit, and suddenly sees that most of the mourners are very old people.

Erm, the way you and I drink warm milk...

SLOW PAN of the dumb-founded MOURNERS. BILLY the GHOST sits on the coffin shaking his head at his brother. Most there think MIKE's deranged. An OLD MAN storms onto the stage and whispers in his ear.

WILLIAM

You're at the wrong bloody funeral you drunken DROPKICK!

MIKE mouths "SORRY" to the mourners and GHOST BILLY grins. As he walks off stage he checks the open casket, noting the name LARRY ADAMS and pauses to face the assembled po-faced Mourners.

MIKE:

I'm really sorry about old LARRY. And he's clearly not my younger brother though that's what he would have looked like at 70. But like they say, Life on this terrestrial chicken-run cum Lunatic asylum is over-fricking-rated, and nobody checks out with a return ticket.Anyway, 86 is a pretty decent innings.

As he passes, he knocks for luck on the coffin lid: Boom! Boom! There's a sudden deafening fart noise and GHOST BILLY jumps as the reanimated Corpse in the coffin sits bolt upright and rubs its eyes. MIKE, and everybody else there, quakes in fright. A WOMAN hurries to embrace the reborn LARRY.

MIKE (ASIDE TO THE SLEEPING BIFF)

Hmm, that can't be good!

GHOST (IRONIC LOOK)
Really? You think, Bro?

LARRY

I believe might have had one too many Sherries the other night...

MIKE stares at him and staggers out into the rain. He pats the pupas it opens one sleepy eye.

MIKE

Yeah I know Mate: this day's only going to get worse.......

GHOST BILLY MAKES AND IRONIC MUGGING CLOWN FACE

8 INT. CREMATORIUM CHAPEL 2.DAY 8

Moments later MIKE enters the right Chapel where they're all waiting impatiently. Some look from him to each other, confirming that MIKE looks wasted. He winces as he passes his tearful sister-in-law CARLY (50) and teenage TWINS JOSH and SARAH (17) in the front row. .

MIKE

I never imagined I'd have to be giving my younger BROTHER's eulogy. And unlike mine will be, he didn't need to rent a crowd.

He looks up and meets the gaze of middle-aged brunette JENN, at the back, and freezes in mid-speech for a few seconds. She gives him a constrained smile.

> I tried to write something special but only managed a bunch of clichés: and that's just won't cut it. So, what I can and will
> do, is show you a short film I made about BILLY'S earlier life. He was a terrific husband and father to Carly, Josh and Sarah, and a fantastic Stuntman, so you know he wasn't afraid of very much, that I can recall; with exception of public speaking and …and, I can't believe I'm saying this, because the only other things he feared were crap from aeroplane toilets or space junk falling on his head! Now that's some scary ju ju… but given he was one of the most accident-prone guys in this galaxy…well, I don't have any other words, so I hope this short film I made about what happened to him at 13 will make you smile and honour his memory. R.I.P BILLY THE KID.

He signals a friend near a projector at the back and heads for the exit, switching off the Chapel lights as he goes. CLOSE on GHOST BILLY fighting total confusion about his situation as he cusses GOD.

BILLY

> So now what's my frickin' motivation, HUEY? (God) He looks through a window at the sky and shakes his fist but the gesture is met by a disturbing peel of approaching thunder.
> Ermmmm. Another fine frickin' mess you've gotten me into. Did anyone ever tell you you've got a sick sense of humour, HUEY, you omniscient SOB?

Even louder thunder now really shuts him up and scares him.

9 EXT. CREMATORIUM.DAY

MIKE sits under a big pepper tree, staring out at the relentless rain. BIFF growls in his sleep. Inside the Chapel the film starts. MIKE's voice narrates.

10 SCENE. CARPARK AT THE RACETRACK

PERCY helps EDDY to the car, as he's under the weather

11 EXT. MELBOURNE INTERNATIONAL AIRPORT. MORNING

DISSOLVE TO BRIGHT DAYLIGHT.

THOMAS MERRIMAN, a chubby Academic 20-year-old and wearing a GROUCHO MARX hand puppet as a glove, emerges from the BEA Arrival lounge wearing headphones and carrying a laptop and a compact futuristic-looking sound contraption.
PAN TO:
GONERIL KINGSTON (20) wears dramatic black clothes and dark GOTH makeup. She emerges through the American Airlines Arrival Gate looking worn-out and cranky. She's trouble on a stick.
CUT TO

12 INT/EXT SPENCER STREET STATION MELBOURNE.DAY

SONNY (MOSHE) LEVI a solid young Jewish MALE steps confidently out of a luxury Greyhound Bus carrying a guitar case. The Sign in the front window of the bus reads: Brisbane-Melbourne.

13 INT. MELBOURNE AIRPORT

BUI HUONG (luminescent 21-year-old VIETNAMESE girl-woman) emerges with a bunch of people from the AIR VIETNAM ARRIVALS GATE. PAN TO MINH ZIE GONG, (35, stocky, goatee and short but powerful looking VIETNAMESE MAN) follows her at a distance. He looks as if he's on a mission.

14 EXT.DAY.CREMATORIUM CAR PARK. DAY

MIKE' still under the dripping tree sipping from his flask. He looks at the chapel at loud applause as the film finishes. HIS POV: Umbrellas spring up as MOURNERS emerge and hurry to their cars. His sister in law CARLY and twins SARAH and JOSH approach and hug him. They're all raw and CARLY gives him a sad smile and holds his hand. BILLY'S sad but proud and impressed by his family.

SARAH

Great film UNCLE MIKE. You did our Dad proud in there.!

JOSH (ABOUT TO LOSE IT)

I'll sure miss his laugh... and his politically incorrect jokes. So, I guess you'll have to be the one who takes me to one of those STRIPPER, beer and prawn nights Dad promised me for my 18th birthday eh MIKE?

MIKE takes BIFF out and holds him out for them.

MIKE

Would either of you like to keep this little bloke? I got him for BILLY and you guys before the, accident. His name's BIFF!

SARAH

I will! He's a Cutie pie.

BIFF pees on MIKE'S hands. They're grateful for the de-stressing. SARAH cradles BIFF as they leave and he washes his hands in the downpour.

15 EXT. CREMATORIUM CARPARK. DAY

The other WOMAN from the CHAPEL now approaches with a younger WOMAN.

JENNIFER SMART (HUGGING HIM)

Hello YOU! Been such a long time!

MIKE (DEADPAN, LOOKING AT HIS WATCH)

24 years in 7 minutes' time, actually.

JENNIFER (JENN)

We saw the funeral notice in the paper. The service went as well as you could hope for. Cold comfort I know. But I really did like your short film just now:That was BILLY to a tee: And he'd have loved it; and loved you the more for making it.

JENN looks as if she's going to tell him something important but visibly thinks better of it.

JENN

So, um, MICHAEL O'LEARY, let me now introduce you to my DAUGHTER WENDY! She's a Drama Grad and would be Director. She'll be assisting me at the ACADEMY part time. By the way, did you hear some industry gossips have already christened our new establishment THE ALLEN SMITHEE ACADEMY! (SLY GRIN)

MIKE (SHAKING HEAD)

Whoa! And our new workplace is starting to sound like a MAFIA employment network!

WENDY approaches him shaking his hand warmly.

WENDY

Nice to finally meet you. I enjoyed your film just now about your brother as well! And I specially loved the "WHISTLING JANE" film you made back in the late 80's. The little GIRL in that was a sensational actor and that story really moved me.

MICK.

That's generous. Thank you. So, how's your Ex, JENN? How IS Mr BRYCE "HOLLYWOOD" SLOANE after all these years?

He's somewhat under the weather now and not mindful about WENDY'S possible feelings about her father.

JENN (REPRIMANDING, EVASIVE)

Well he's still WENDY'S DAD, for starters!! Anyway, you and I both will find out over champers at the Black-tie soiree tonight. But you're already off to an unwise early start I see! As far as I know he's the same old Hollywood BRYCE of yester year. I know it's been decades plus, since you and I have seen each other, but it's been almost 20 years for him and WENDY and me as well. You must have known we divorced after only five years.

WENDY's uncomfortable, and walks out of hearing.
JENN glances at her daughter, who's turned away.

JENN (WHISPERING, CONSPIRATORIAL)

But what can I say? We both know what an incurable pants man he was, and his Los Angeles casting-couch always had a desperate queue. Even WENDY rarely hears
from him. And you need to know that his other daughter JULIE, WENDY's half-sister, whom he had with that FRENCH ACTRESS ANNIE FARDEAU will actually be in your class.

MIKE

JESUS H Nepotism on a stick! Is there ANY freaking humanoid we DON'T know starting with us at that FRACKING FOOL NEDDY KELLY's Film ACADEMY?

JENN (GRINNING)

I'll have you know that our "Benefactor" and Boss is not just a Natural Gas Windbag, he did well in GARBAGE DISPOSAL and "upmarket" Porn Publishing as well. But I guess you're right: it's getting exactly like that. So, Master O'LEARY, we'll be seeing a lot of each other again from now on. You still up for the hard grind of teaching bushy-tailed Undergrads again?

MIKE

Don't have a Fracking choice now do I JENN? I have to pay rent like everyone else.

JENN shrugs as WENDY wanders back checking her watch.

JENN

Well, we'd best be going. WENDY has to meet JULIE for the first time today, as well as assist with Film

JENN(CONT.)

auditions, for some extra cash…erm..
MIKE"S face begs the question and JENN winces with your flamboyant old UNI peer,DORIAN MOORE FOUCAULT. DORIAN has financed two new ARTHOUSE Films

MIKE shakes his head but looks vaguely amused.

MIKE

ARTHOUSE! Don't you mean OUT HOUSE?

JENN (WENDY REJOINS THEM)

Yet he has an uncanny knack of somehow winning grants and funding his films: and you've "gotta" admire his chutzpah, though I know he's not one of your favourite people

MIKE

Sure he's part egocentric, and possibly certifiable, but I guess I've kind of grown to admire his gobsmacking delusions of grandeur and his getting stuff made.

JENN:

Just as well! Because he'll be joining as at the ACADEMY as well as BRYCE –
MIKE MAKES A SHOCKED FACE
At least till our first International Film Festival just before Christmas, and maybe even past then. You have to admit though, a Festival of that standing is pretty damn exciting! The cash prizes are already attracting some big names that went to SUNDANCE. We'll have our work cut out for us though getting students to write, shoot and edit

JENN(CONT.)

three decent quality ten minute films and a 60 minute TV pilot in 19 weeks. It won't be any kind of stroll in the park.

MIKE

It's actually only your Ex – my new Boss, I'm concerned about.

MIKE LOOKS like all his Hell days have come at once.

WENDY

We need to leave, MUM..

MIKE shakes WENDY'S hand and kisses JENN on the cheek. He watches them go and suddenly discovers a smelly sandwich in his pocket which he punts into a garbage bin like a pro football player kicking a field goal.

16 EXT.ROAD AND AN OLD CITY THEATRE.DAY 16

JENN double parks and WENDY jumps out and heads into the Theatre.

17 EKAFTTWA FUNCTIONS CENTRE AFTERNOON.17

DISSOLVES show many people still busily preparing for the big night.

18 SC.EXT. PICTURESQUE BIKE TRAIL YARRA RIVER DISSOLVE TO

A young Aboriginal man on a designer bicycle and in a designer Tracksuit, cycles jauntily fast along the River-bank path.

18 B SCENE.INT.EXT SPENCER ST. STATION.DAY

BERNADETTE HAWKINS (21) cheerful personable country girl alights from an Interstate Fast train with heavy suitcases.

19 INT. LATE 19TH CENTURY HERITAGE THEATRE – DAY19

The setting is a beautiful and stately VICTORIAN-ERA THEATRE and MOVIE complex in Melbourne's C.B.D

19 B THEATRE FOYER. DAY

A few dozen cinema PATRONS line up for movie tickets. WENDY SMART stands near the compact wine bar checking her Mobile. FROM HER POV she looks at a photo and suddenly recognizes JULIE SLOANE (21, intelligent looking attractive silver blonde) entering the foyer.

WENDY

So, you ARE real after all! Finally, we get to meet. AND you're just as pretty as...

WENDY gives her a big loving hug.

as pretty as your photos, JULIE. It's lovely having a sister, or at least a half-sister. I wish we'd met much earlier in our lives though.

Taciturn JULIE openly responds to her warmth.

JULIE

Me too, WENDY! You look beautiful. I guess that means we must both have very good-looking MOTHERS then.

They both laugh at the joke about BRYCE'S ordinary looks.

WENDY

Anyhoo, we might have to save the "getting-to-know-yous" for later. DORIAN's about to start auditions, so best not be late.
I'm helping him with a bit of casting for extra cash. Can't promise you a role,as he makes all the decisions. I would try to influence him but he already knows we're related and who our father is. And they've never particularly liked each other....
Anyhow, auditioning is always good practice, so break a leg in there. Don't let DORIAN get to you, either: He means well(WENDY CONT) but sometimes he just can't help being high maintenance. See you at the launch this evening and we'll have a few celebratory drinks, yeah?

She watches JULIE head up the stairs to the PLAY THEATRE

20 SCENE.INT.THEATRE.DAY 20

Seen from a bird's eye P.O.V from the "Bleacher Stalls", a portly, shortish, effete, and apparent EGOMANIAC, struts and frets his "hour" upon the stage: He paces up and down glorying in his power. In front of him are assembled a motley group of ACTORS sitting in all manner of poses in the front rows. They all watch him effortlessly appearing to hang on his every word (Their being actors) although sly reaction snapshot POVs of many of them suggests they think his self-infatuation is borderline Lunacy.

DORIAN now moves to stand at WENDY's side as she dons her Casting Agent hat.

WENDY (VERY SUBTLY IRONIC)

Hi everyone. I'm WENDY SMART and I'll be assisting with the Casting today. First, I'd like to thank you all for arriving punctually.
Today will be the first of six AUDITION sessions for the two INDIE feature films (CONT) DORIAN MOORE-FOUCAULT will be making soon after New Year's Day and up till July next year.

CLOSE: She looks pained for a moment and there is a fleeting Reaction shot suggesting she considers him a flouncing egotistical S.O.B

WENDY

As any of you who have not been cryogenically-frozen for the past two decades would know, DORIAN has won the coveted "Un Certain Regard" Awards at the MEKNES, ULAN BATOR, and SOUTH CAMDEN film Festivals two years running …

CUT TO:

CLOSE ON an earnest late-teenage YOUTH sprouting the beginning of a goatee. The youth glances from WENDY to his copy of Actors' "BIBLE", "STANISLAVSKY and the Art of Acting". The Book looks as though he's been sleeping on it and possibly eating it or driving over it for years

PAN TO CCU. A genteel-poor looking actor (65, bow tie, tattered tweed jacket, leather elbow protectors and frayed white DUNLOP gym shoes) is reading a Japanese SF comic featuring pneumatic-breasted alien females with vulpine heads. He's eating DORITOS over his dog-eared notes page and spilling some on the floor.

PAN TO WIDE there's an eclectic looking mix of strung out, eccentric and unemployed looking male and female ACTORS aged between 18 and 75. AND one extremely heavily made-up and alarmingly precocious GIRL of 14 going on 25.
Some pore over scripts, declaim and recite under their breath, memorizing key voices. Some cross themselves. Most perform quirky superstitious pre-audition mantras. They read "Cosmopolitan", "HQ" and "TV Week", and one criminal looking man studies HIS LAPTOP. CLOSE: His screen displays graphics of the floor plans of a local bank and security guard figures in strategic positions and the curser moves around the images showing locations of security cameras and times of opening and closing.
CUT TO: WOLFGANG HORSCHILD (22, muscle-bound stylish Aryan and lascivious) also a comic reader, who ogles JULIE SLOANE sitting in front of him.

WENDY

…..Moreover, MISTER MOORE FOUCAULT has recently garnered nineteen French nentalIndependent Best Film Award nominations for his bravely dark urban oeuvre, "DUET FOR A MUTE , which garnered $144,000 after 59 weeks on 172 screens.

WOLFGANG (TO JULIE)

DORIAN MOOR- FFFOUC.? What in the verld kind off name is that? And how in the name of BEALZEBUB may I spell it?

JULIE half turns around and smilingly spells it out for him.

JULIE(WITH SOME VITRIOL)

Well DORIAN'S after the Narcissistic Devil-dealing OSCAR WILDE character DORIAN GREY: You know, his portrait got nastier and older as he went on and on looking like BRAD PITT !

JULIE

Then there's M.O.O.R.E , HYPHEN FOUCAULT, which I choose TO pronounce: FOOKER: It's French/Moroccan/ Irish. It's said his Mom was a snake charmer from MARRAKESH and his DAD was, um, charmed, legless drunk, and a long way from TIPPERARY at the time – and suddenly, it's midnight at the Oasis and he demands she teach him one on one belly-dancing. Then, BANG! Nine months later a hospital ward curtain-call and there you have him in the Flesh - D.M.F, Dune Messiah of the Independent Film world.

WOLFGANG scratches his head at her idioms.

WENDY (READING ALOUD)

I must also add that it says in this magazine article that DORIAN has been named in several European CINEASTE Publications as among the top 100 Auteur Directors on the planet. CUT TO:

DORIAN "modestly' raises his hand to cut the flattery.

JULIE

But which planet? METHANOS MINOR? Auteur's a poseur French word for a film maker claiming to have a unique stylistic vision for filmic story telling.

WOLFGANG doesn't appear to have a clue what she's talking about

Some Auteurs think they're cleverer than MARK TWAIN, EUGENE O'NEILL or theBRONTE SISTERS or whoever wrote the story in the first place. Lots of their films feature images like lingering shots of feet, toes with blackberry jam

JULIE(CONT.)

between them, or some-such, because they've got a thing about tinea imagery in VIRGINIA WOOLF, or fire - think pyromania: so if you're watching burning bushes, long-hair catching fire from a dropped lighter, or Blazing Saddles under the butts of the four horsemen of the Apocalypse you'll know it's Auteurs at work! It's all about sex of course. Cinema Academics love the Auteurs as it gives them something intellectually contrived to lecture about and write about to fill their own creative voids.

WOLFGANG

Ach zo! I understand you now

JULIE

Lots of the words are from the French language as well. Academics love that too. It's pretentious, sets them apart, like Latin for Lawyers and German for Doktors: it helps some Film makers mystify unoriginal crap. Hmm, I give you Exhibit A: "HOMAGE !": Moore-Foucault types call it a tribute, but basically, it's just a rip off of some other poor earlier bugger's original work….a bit like someone sending you a photo of your new car after they steal it.

She finally turns right around to fully face WOLFGANG

My name's JULIE SLOANE. You might have heard of my Dad? BRYCE SLOANE? WOLFGANG SHRUGS HIS SHOULDERS. Anyhoo, I'm auditioning for both films today and I'm also starting a World class film course tomorrow: at Edward Kelly THE Third ACADEMY OF FILM, TELEVISION AND THEATRE in South Yarra.

WOLFGANG (BLOCKED NOSE, FLU-AFFECTED, ARROGANT)

Amazing!! Das ist gut! Zo am I!

She's taken aback by this. Her face says "How in Hell?

WOLFGANG

Zo, you Really DON'T KNOW who I am, do you?

JULIE (CHEEKY CYNICAL)

No, but my DAD knows a Doctor who specialises in Amnesia I could refer you too.

He feigns a mock sneer and sees she's a match for him.

WOLFGANG

I, am WOLFGANG HORSCHILD..

JULIE

Yeah, I thought you sounded a little hoarse.

WOLFGANG

Ja, I HAF A COLT! I am From Hamburg and Buenos Aries..

She studies him for a second visibly wondering if his comic pronunciation of "COLT" FOR COLD might have been an execrable pun, but instantly dismisses the possibility)

> I too will be at EDWARD KELLY SCHOOL even if I get film actor role. She's shocked for a moment as to how he could get in. My Mother, is HISPANIC ARGENTINIAN -
> But maybe you have heard of mein FARTER..er Father : He is the BAVARIAN DIEDERICH HORSCHILD, Billionaire FOUNDER AND

WOLFGANG(CONT.)

OWNER OF HORSCHILD SPORTSWEAR..and HORSCHILD SHOES

JULIE nods in relief at this clarification. Only MONEY would get WOLFGANG into the course, her face says.

JULIE

SO I GUESS THAT MEANS HORSCHILD SHOES IS A store where FOALS rush in?

She grins at her pathetic joke but he ignores it

WOLFGANG

MEIN FARTER vill even fund my first feature film he has said.

JULIE stares at him in disbelief for a second

> That is if I pass, of course. So, JULIE, If you are auditioning for each film you must be a real Actress

JULIE (CYNICAL)

Yeah I am a REAL ACTOR alright. Or "THESPIAN"

She makes little inverted commas with her fingers

JULIE

Because like 90% of us I must also occasionally have to spend some of my days or nights as a waitress or running KARAOKE and TRIVIA nights at Pubs, or modelling in lingerie sections of Department stores. One of my girl-friend Thespians is a Chinese-Australian and she even does some occasional Lap Dancing for decaying Geeks with weak hearts at a sleazy nightclub. Not surprisingly the old COOTS

JULIE(CONT.)

call her the ORIENTAL EXPRESS. Club's called The OCCIDENTAL.

WOLFGANG

Ze Nightclub is.. Accidental?

JULIE

No: More like Incidental. We all do it - to keep the wolf – well, not the WOLFGANG necessarily - from the Door, and in the
name of research for our Method Acting, in order to keep it real, as they say. Um, you need to know, there will probably be some wise guys at the ACADEMY who'll probably want to nickname you "PACK"

WOLFGANG looks in his dictionary and makes a "Please clarify" face.

JULIE

Well a gang is a pack! WOLFGANG equals Wolf pack… so, Pack! Or WOLFIE

WOLFGANG (REMINISCENT OF HITLER RANT)

NEIN! NEIN! NEIN! No one will be calling me that Fraulein Senorita.

Something in his tone tell her he's not joking
DORIAN's now front and centre stage gesturing theatrically.

DORIAN

So without more ado, my first film this year will be "THE YOUNG HANNIBAL".
Both FILMS will be highly visceral, and while I'm hoping to attach actors like GUY PEARCE and JULIA LUIS DREYFUS as leads, I intend using some new faces too - hopefully some of you, for a few key

DORIAN(CONT.)

roles, as well as leathery old stagers with marquee value, like DULCIE FUDGE and EDDY WACKETT. But my first film is my personal FAVE. I'm calling it "THE YOUNG HANNIBAL"

DORIAN'S stoked by his own brilliance. JULIE yawns and raises her hand.

JULIE

Do you plan to cast HAMILCAR BARCA'S son HANNIBAL with an eye patch DORIAN? And given that breed of African elephants his soldiers rode on are extinct now, I was wondering if you plan to use Asian elephants? CUT TO

WENDY makes and "Oh! Oh!" Face, as if JULIE has shot herself in the foot: With an Elephant gun! DORIAN raises an imperious eyebrow.

DORIAN

Not HANNIBAL the frickin' CARTHAGINIAN General, LOVIE...!

JULIE (WHISPERING TO WOLFGANG)

"Whoops! No frickin relation.

DORIAN

I'm talking DOCTOR HANNIBAL FRICKIN' LECTOR of course. I see him as the precocious seventeen year old HEAD of the DEBATING TEAM at the exclusive SAINT ANAESTHESIA'S ACADEMY in
Upmarket Melbourne. It's set back in 1969 during the first Moon landing. Plot-wise,

He draws images in the air with his hands

> A few below-par TEACHERS and a SCHOOL NURSE begin disappearing, and subsequently the general standard of food in the school CAFETERIA improves markedly, almost overnight. It culminates with the suspicious disappearance of young HANNIBAL's nemesis, the bullying HEADMASTER DOCTOR SHRIKE, who incorrectly - and fatally in this case - gets DORIAN his just desserts, when he misuses the word "Incunabula" at the Academy's Speech Night. Consequently he's served up at the ACADEMY's Founders' Day celebratory dinner for Staff
> and Parents, comprised of all the social elite and Nabobs of BRIGHTON and BEAUMARIS in attendance. The Dinner is a kind of GOODBYE MISTER CHIPS with mixed vegetables and gravy if you will ...but more of that later.

He paces the stage theatrically daubing his brow with a kerchief.

DORIAN

> These films already have pre sales in Chad, Assyria, Moldova and Guatemala, which means you'll be reaching important markets that could help define your careers. So, let's cut to the chase: My other FEATURE FILM will be "ALL OUT OF KILTS", a surreal Modernist reinterpretation of MACBETH and 11th century Scottish Politics, but featuring instead, battling DESIGNERS in the RAG TRADE in Melbourne's TOORAK and DOUBLE BAY in Sydney.

He's wide eyed in anticipation of the audience reaction. JULIE mouths the word "HOMAGE" to WOLFGANG and hurriedly writes some notes. Other actors are suddenly alert

DORIAN

So … let's start with you down there. Erm, JULIA, no JULIE…

DORIAN Consults notes and photo sheets and he almost sneers as he makes the connection as to who her father is. MIKE is watching all this with a grin from a concealed vantage point in a dark alcove. BILLY'S GHOST also watches from nearby and shakes his head in amused disbelief at DORIAN

DORIAN

I'd like you to read for the part of JO BETH SCOTT, AKA Lady MAC BETH.

DORIAN

Now, she's recently coerced her Husband MACKA, based on MAC BETH, to pass on some poisoned cocaine to the flamboyant JOHN GALLIANO-type, THANE FIFE, one of his major designer rivals in the country. So, she's having trouble sleeping: Your motivation is guilt - BUT you could tap into your experiences of P.M.T:The P of course meaning Permanent, in order to extract every morsel of ringing emotion from the scene.

JULIE gives him a "looks can kill" glare and glances at WENDY, watching from the wings. SHE is similarly livid. JULIE passes the notes she's written over to WOLFGANG. CLOSE on the NOTES shows a dialogue-improvised scene between JO BETH and MACKA

JULIE

You might want to glance at these notes WOLFIE. I wrote your part just in case.

He takes her advice and starts studying the notes.
On Stage, JULIE knows the play and transforms into Mad LADY "JO BETH", launching into an abridged version of the famous soliloquy, and transfixing her audience. JULIE stares at her hands in horror at and rubs them as she speaks.

JULIE

Out damned spot! Out I say! One two; why then 'tis time to do it. Hell is murky! Fie my Lord. THANE FIFE he had a wife, he was trouble, she was strife, and the very bane of his shite-life: but where is she now? What, will these hands ne'r be Clean? All the perfumes of SOUTH MELBOURNE will not sweeten this little hand.

JULIE spies WENDY giving her the thumbs up, as she is clearly very impressed, but DORIAN interrupt

DORIAN

Passable! Passable! But now for a real tester: Improvisation - IMPROV CHERIE! So, YOU there

He consults the call sheets

DORIAN

WOLFGANG HORSCHILD! I love it! A bolter!

WOLFGANG almost gallops onto the stage. He's got a sense of humour it seems.

WOLFGANG

Could I but look into the seeds of time and say will she live or swoon and pine,

> JO BETH
>
> so withered now stands bereft not within the prospect of belief; and forsooth, what breasts through yonder window break!

Her face shows she know she's "been had" by WOLFGANG's clever Eurotrash impersonation.

> DORIAN
>
> Bravo young man for a sterling effort. Bravo indeed. You will definitely receive further consideration. I'd also like to thank you JENNA. I think you have some potential and your understanding of the Craft, would be much improved after a year at one of the new Acting courses being run around town these days.

His patronizing attitude makes an unnecessary enemy

> JULIE
>
> It's JULIE. My name is JULIE, DORIAN, not JENNA or JEDDA! JULIE SLOANE

> DORIAN
>
> Of course it is. Just leave your resume on the way out CHERIE

WENDY looks at JULIE and points her finger to her head as if it's a pistol. JULIE manages a grateful smile for the gesture of support.

21 INT. MEDIA LAUNCH EDWARD KELLY FILM ACADEMY. NIGHT 21

It's all happening at the glittering function at the new wing of the ACADEMY. The four Key Film and Acting staff are all seen in huge photographic portraits (each of them in their early thirties when in their prime) which are projected onto the large screen at the back of the stage. The PORTRAITS of the Twelve Students of the first intake are in smaller sized frames and placed next to those of their LECTURERS. Milling guests at the Black tie and evening-wear shindig drink champagne from flutes and eat expensive nibbles served by young women who look like high end Call Girls or swimsuit models. EDDY KELLY himself is rubbing shoulders with power brokers though looks a bit like a spiv in a monkey suit. His slick Pro Vice Chancellor PERCY (PERCE) SLATER is working the room like a "well oiled" gigolo.

22 SCENE.INT. FUNCTIONS-CENTRE. KELLY FILM ACADEMY. NIGHT

Several of the feted STUDENTS are very nervous and drinking too quickly. They are a mixed bunch from diverse cultural backgrounds EDDY KELLY schmoozes with the GLITTERATI and LITTERATI and introduces his "Lecturers" to the guests and to some half-soused MEDIA REPS from TV Networks BEHAVING LIKE PIGS AT A TROUGH. There's also a couple of famous look alike TV personalities stuffing food in their pockets and swilling champers like it's lemonade. And there's a lot of testosterone and egos flying around.
SLOW PAN from the youthful portraits of the Key staff to their 50 year old selves in the crowd

23 SCENE.INT.FUNCTIONS CENTRE.NIGHT

JENN plays nice as the Peacekeeper BUT has her work cut out as MIKE and BRYCE SLOANE still loathe each other, and SLOANE has open contempt for DORIAN. SLOANE wears a very expensive suit. He's thin and pasty faced and has an expensive hair piece blended with a short pony tail and pearly white teeth caps. He drinks like it's a race.

SLOANE (PHONEY KIWI-AMERICAN ACCENT)

Looking Foxy Tonight, JENNIFER! I can see my second girl, but where's our older progeny.

JENN

I doubt you'd recognize her given you only contact her once in a blue moon: you didn't remember her 13th, 16th or 21st birthdays and never replied to most of her little girl letters. You broke her heart.

SLOANE (NOT EVEN LISTENING)

I spy the golden child.

He sees JULIE conversing with an older guest.

Where BE SHE of the viper tongue. Pity she wasn't more like JULIE.. Now that one is a genuine chip off the old block!

SLOANE goads MIKE. JENN fights to remain polite and nods at their daughter WENDY conversing with students

But daughter number one, well, between you and me and the C.N.N Network, it was one wild and WOOLLY night in the WINDY CITY when JENN conceived the feisty one! Hence the name. WENDY!

He's rubbing it in with MIKE and it soon becomes clear they've also been rivals for JENN in the past. DORIAN now joins them.

JENN was another one that got away eh MIKE? Bit like your Movie Directing career, yeah?

MIKE

Well at least I didn't sell out to fringe Hollywood to make Porn flicks and C Grade SCHLOCK for illiterate and priapic teenagers! Yeah, BRYCE T SLOANE, still a Poster Boy for haemorrhoid suppositories after all these years. What A shock!

They're about to step outside. People near them are uncomfortable. DORIAN and JENN step between them. PERCY too is concerned.

JENN

You puerile narcissist bastards! Carrying on like that in this place at THIS time. YOU might have plenty of Job offers BRYCE, but I'll be 51 in a month and I need this position. Can't you just do something for WENDY and me for once in bloody your life, and behave like a grown-up man here tonight. And you're hardly any better, MIKE!

They quieten down and SLOANE sulks off towards the STUDENT group

24 SCENE. INT. ACADEMY FUNCTIONS CENTRE. NIGHT

EDDY KELLY and PERCY SLATER, the chameleon VICE CHANCELLOR) schmooze with wealthy guests. PERCY stands on stage.

PERCY (CONVINCING POSH VOICE)

Good evening.. and welcome. Distinguished guests, ladies and gentlemen, new students, and new esteemed staff

He nods almost ironically at the four key STAFF

PERCY(CONT.)

WELCOME to the opening of the EDWARD KELLY ACADEMY OF FILM, TELEVISION AND ACTING. So without further ado I would now like to introduce you to the FOUNDER AND owner of the ACADEMY, iconic MINING and Publishing giant, EDWARD KELLY the Third.

Cameras appear. There's polite applause. POVs of audience faces show KELLY is not held in the highest regard by some Society Guests. He's a rough diamond to be sure. PERCY whispers in his ear before he heads for the rostrum.

> Give these egotistical Dick-heads an earful of the real blarney, MATE.

KELLY (READING SOMEWHAT POORLY)

Many thanks PERCY SLATER, our illustrious Vice Chancellor. And a special welcome, to State Governor PENELOPE FOWLER

He nods at an alcoholic looking red faced FEMALE "dignitary" with a large Polynesian MINDER (lover?) as company

> and also to Senator FRED MC CARTNEY

FRED looks one beer short of a triple bypass emergency.

KELLY

IMPORTANT GUESTS and members of the MEDIA...

From BRYCE's POV, three women who might be Dominatrices, are a colourful but inappropriate addition to this Schmooze-athon. PERCY SLATER'S face suggests he has organized this.

> **KELLY**
>
> It is with great pleasure I now declare
> this magnificent new State of the Art Film Making
> and Film Business Teaching facility open. And to
> really launch it, I can now tell you all that we will be
> holding our first BUSHRANGER INTERNATIONAL
> FILM FESTIVAL just before Christmas in just under
> five months' time, with some very rich prizes.
> PERCY's guaranteed this Festival will really put our
> Institution on the International Film Circuit map
> overnight and cement our instant world rating
> Academic status. So without more ado I will now take
> the opportunity to introduce you to four of our
> illustrious key staff.

He gestures to MIKE, DORIAN, JENN and SLOANE as they mount the stage and stand in front of and below their respective youthful photos)

> AND THEY ARE: Esteemed Writer-Directors
> DORIAN MOORE FOUCAULT, MIKE O'LEARY
> and BRYCE SLOANE - BRYCE will Also be Head of
> SCHOOL; And brilliant Stage, Film and Television
> actress and former Golden Globe Best Actress
> winner,
> JENNIFER SMART, who will be teaching the Acting
> and Theatre Arts courses with assistance from her
> daughter WENDY for the first intake of Australian
> and globally hand-picked STUDENTS

He nods at STUDENTS mounting the dais.

> **KELLY**
>
> The students then, are: GONERIL KINGSTON,
> from OREGON

Some GUESTS are alarmed as GONERIL (Dressed like Vampire Bordello MADAM) stares them down. She also carries a riding crop for no apparent reason

> **KELLY**
>
> U.S.A; STEVE SANDERS, from Dublin Ireland;

An open can of Guinness can be seen protruding from his back pocket.

> **EX WALLABY FOOTBALLER JUSTIN MORROW**

He sports a monster shiner

> **CAMBRIDGE UNIVERSITY HISTORY MEDALIST, THOMAS MERRIMAN**

MERRIMAN is having a panic attack and using an inhaler. He looks ready to throw up on his Cambridge blazer.

> CANADIAN singer and model STEPHANIE RHODES

Some sleazy male guests are visually salivating over her

> TEHERAN and ABU DHABI SOCIALITE AMAL HOSSEINI

She's dressed like a princess from the ARABIAN-NIGHTS with curling slippers, veils & puffed-Sheer pants.

> BERNADETTE HAWKINS, Country singer and swine whisperer from GULLENGUBBA NSW

She's painfully shy and dressed like TAMMY WYNETTE at a NASHVILLE hoedown in 1970

KELLY

BUI HUONG, from University of Hanoi;

CUT TO her secret minder Minh in the crowd taking photos secretively.

> Exciting new Composer SONNY MOSHE LEVI from Queensland, Indigenous Student of the year WALTER HARROWER..FROM SYDNEY; WOLFGANG HORSCHILD FROM BUENOS AIRES AND MUNCHEN..and maybe HOGAN's HEROES? (MUTTERED)

WOLFGANG wears a Colonel Klink monocle and makes a totally inappropriate V for Victory sign to the crowd;

> and the ACADEMY'S Inaugural Scholarship winner, JULIE SLOANE, from New Zillund and SANTA MONICA CALIFORNIA.

There's solid applause for all of them. As the STUDENTS descend the stairs SLOANE nods at a surly supercilious BESUITED streak of misery who stands in the path of shy portly BRIT student MERRIMAN, affable Irish American MUSICIAN SANDERS and cheerful, clever Composer MOSHE. For a few seconds the MAN blocks their way after they leave the stage.

EASTER

> So, you're great new hopes for World Cinema? I don't think so.

He allows them to pass and MERRIMAN glances back over his shoulder at EASTER with a deflated look.

SCENE.INT.UNIVERSITY FUNCTIONS CENTRE. .NIGHT

MIKE notices this exchange and watches MERRIMAN looking painfully alone and gawky at the bar. He already seems ostracized from the rest of the more confident student group so MIKE wanders over to yarn to him. JENNIFER and WENDY are in conversation with other STUDENTS and BENEFACTORS but both notice him showing his caring side.

WENDY

He seems a nice man.

JENN

He has his moments

WENDY

Did you and MIKE ever date, MUM?

JENN takes a glass of wine from a passing waiter

JENN

They were different times then WEN. Can I get you another champagne Sweetie?

She looks away and WENDY studies him for a moment.

25 SCENE. INT. BAR AREA .FUNCTIONS CENTRE NIGHT.

MIKE

Hi there TOM! I'm MIKE, one of your TEACHERS.

MERRIMAN

Yes Sir I'm very pleased to meet you. It's THOMAS, by the way.

MIKE

And I've never been officially knighted either. So what did LURCH over there have to say to you? I saw you react to him.

MERRIMAN

Is he someone important?

MIKE (TIPSY AGAIN NOW)

In his own mind he's the LOVE CHILD of STANLEY KUBRICK and MERRIL STREEP. In my mind, however, he's an auto-coprotaphagic - it means he eats his own shite - Lounge Lizard with an ego the size of the NULLABOR PLAIN.

MERRIMAN is embarrassed and amused in equal measure.

MERRIMAN

He said he didn't think any of us would amount to much as Film makers.

MIKE

Did he now? We'll have to prove his judgement isn't worth an ingrown wart on E Bay then, won't we?

THOMAS grins as if there may actually be a small window of hope he might fit in at this School.

26 INT.SMART NEW BAR ENTERTAINMENT AREA MELBOURNE.NIGHT

Some of the STUDENTS as well as MIKE, JENN and WENDY have kicked on after the Function at a TRENDY CITY BAR. SLOANE is there too, sitting in a far corner doing a line for two attractive BIMBOS and using his Film PRODUCER-DIRECTOR shtick to charm them. At SLOANE'S table the two much younger WOMEN seem open to anything if he'll give them a part in something. He tells them he's casting for a comeback film.

CHRISTIE

So about that Film you're going to make BRYCE ..um..

SLOANE

THE FORSAKEN HARLOT?

CHRISTIE

Yeah that's it! And the Blonde Bombshell part you thought I might be right for?

SLOANE

Her name is TOULA BAZULAS. She's GREEK!

CHRISTIE

So does she put out for the STALKER before, or after he shtups her MOTHER?

SLOANE lets his guard down for a second and stares at her in disbelief. Without answering her he now focuses on the other WOMAN, a lithe brunette. CHRISTIE looks desperate and starts Texting someone: ANYONE

SLOANE

So, REBECCA, how long have you been having singing lessons?

REBECCA

About an hour each timeHe's stunned by her as well and picks up a full champagne bottle and swigs from it. When he glances at the STUDENT group he's suddenly aware BUI HUONG is staring at him. He gives her a sly wink and eavesdrops on his companions prattling into their Mobiles.

27 INT.KELLY FILM ACADEMY STUDENT ACCOMMODATION WING.

When the AFTER FUNCTION end STUDENTS return to their new very upmarket rooms in the secure HOSTEL Wing. They all sit in the large lounge and recreation area intent on properly meeting each other, but when MERRIMAN falls asleep in his chair and starts snoring like a chainsaw, they all start yawning and head off for their well-appointed individual rooms. WOLFGANG, who is wearing a pseudo Viking helmet with horns, is the second last to go and wakes THOMAS.

WOLFGANG

Time to rendezvous with the SANDMAN THOMAS. You are bunking next door to me, so I am hoping you can stop your snoring now so I am not having to be inserting two socks in your nostrils after lights **out..!**

THOMAS is wide eyed now and not sure whether or not he is serious.

28 SCENE.INT.LECTURE AND SEMINAR ROOM. MIKE'S HOME ROOM.DAY

It's DAY 1 and the first full meeting of some STAFF and STUDENTS SEMINAR ROOM 4 substantial in size with one large round table and three smaller rectangular ones. There's a Smart Board and prominent screen at the front as well as HIGH TECH SOTA equipment and so forth.
POSTERS of the Keystone Cops, BUSTER KEATON, HOPALONG CASSIDY, JIMMY STEWART AND DONNA REED, WATERWORLD, , Gone with the Wind, 12 Angry Men, A CLOCKWORK ORANGE, THE MAGNIFICENT AMBERSONS,Marilyn Monroe and Jane Russell, CINERAMA,BATMAN BEGINS, La Belle au Bois Dormant,

Irma la Douche, KNIFE in the WATER, BEING THERE, THE PIANO, RIPLEY FROM ALIEN and Cate Blanchett and Avatar, INTERSTELLAR and Lord of the Rings festoon the walls. The STUDENTS are talking among themselves and waiting. They've clearly been introducing themselves to the group and saying one fact about themselves.

WOLFGANG (STILL IN HIS VIKING HELMET SUSTAINS HIS COMIC ACCENT)

> Jawohl, WOLFGANG from Argentina and MUNCHEN and I haf come here to shoot some sheep, meet and boink some sexy AUSTRALIAN SHEILAS und make movies like ARNOLD SHWARZUND- BEEF-UND-EGGENBURGER ...and, it's time to come clean and tell you I don't really talk like this...sorry JULIE.

The other students laugh. JULIE'S STILL PEEVED FROM THE AUDITION They all turn their heads to listen to the FEMALE GOTH.

GONERIL (DEADPAN))

> My name is GONERIL KINGSTON and I'm American, in case you couldn't tell from my "cockeyed optimism", my hat size, my Free the LAB RATS badge and cobalt blue hair. I've actually lived some eventful years since I was abducted by some over-sexed Pissant ALIENS from the Orion Nebula when I was 14..

They all stare at her. It's deathly quiet till MIKE O'LEARY noisily enters the room.

SCENE.INT. SEMINAR ROOM.DAY

MIKE sits and places student info books on the table checking each

of them against a Register with names& photos and personal
details. BILLY'S GHOST watches everything but seems totally lost

MIKE

Call me ISHMAEL.

AMAL (TO SONNY)

Ishn't ISHMAEL your Hishtorical Homeland right
nesht to PALESHTEIN?

SONNY/MOSHE

I'm an AUSSIE JEW from downtown Brisbane, not
an ISRAELI, DELILAH. So, where DID you park
your pet Dromedary?

AMAL

I prefer two humps to one, BEN HUR, like
my coffee and my boyfriends, so
my camel's a Bactrian, not a Dromedary

WALLY

Erm, I guess we all know "Call me ISHMAEL", is the
opening line of HERMANN MELVILLE'S Great
American novel "MOBY DICK", but I hope that
doesn't make this seminar room the story's Whaling
ship the PEQUOD, and us its doomed CREW. I
hope you're not even vaguely suggesting our dreams
are going to drown here the way theirs did?

MIKE

You're absolutely right Meister HARROWER
that was a very dumb analogy. Can you
give me a more appropriate ship's name
for the Journey we're about to embark on in
this 4th dimension vessel.. THE SS
SEMINAR ROOM NUMBER 4?

He spreads his arms as if the Seminar Room is indeed a vessel. It sounds lame and he has to try harder.

MIKE

For here we will start to navigate our way through the skills, knowledge and the creative savvy required to conceive and capture great Film and Television stories writ large and small. Any other ship names (MIKE) come to mind. I guessed I've milked that analogy ....? I've been out of circulation for a while now and I'm guessing it shows.JENN knocks on the door. He gets up to answer and chat to her as GONERIL answers his question, but fortunately he doesn't hear her.

GONERIL

Other SHIPS he asks! Hmm, how about the Good Ship LOLLIPOP, the wreck of the HESPERUS or the MARY CELESTE?

The other STUDENTS are bemused by her sarcastic attitude.

MERRIMAN (TO SANDERS)

The MARY CELESTE was a ghost ship that sailed the Seven Seas crew-less for decades, erm..

GONERIL

And what's his shtick with that overrated FISH-FEST, "MOBY DICK".
If they sold copies of that book in the SLEEP AID section of PHARMACIES it would put MOGADON and TYLENOL out of business.

JUSTIN

What a crock! It's a timeless mighty tale told by a Master Story Teller.

She glares at him as JENN joins the group with a pile of course pamphlets

MIKE

Class, this is JENN SMART, a terrific and once and future hot stage and film actor who'll be taking you through the performing Arts process this year and next.

JENN (DISTRIBUTES BOOKLETS)

Hi everyone. Don't mind me.
But yes, I shall be taking all of you for ACTING 101 but also, hopefully, some of
you right through to Film, Television and Broadway Fame and Fortune. I'm just here for a meet and greet and to give you these course outlines.

MIKE

So how's about we start with each of you giving us a thumbnail portrait of yourself: who you are, where you're from, your three favourite films and why, and what you'd like
to achieve when, IF and after you graduate from this course. Let's start with …whom?
ALL simultaneously point at GONERIL, saying "HER!!"

JUSTIN

Is there any chance you could go first, ISHMAEL. erm.

MIKE

Okay. ISHMAEL and AHAB were a dumb start. My grey matter's been in hibernation for three years, let's just make it plain old MIKE

JUSTIN

Sure thing MIKE ! A few of us saw your debut feature movie "WHISTLING JANE", that you made when you were only a few years older than we are now, and we reckon it was worthy of OSCAR nomination. I never understood understand why the heck it didn't go gang-busters//

MERRIMAN

My research leads me to believe it's critical and Box Office failure can be attributed to the malice of a painfully biased and puffed-up review by an absurdly influential internationally-Syndicated-Film Critic: seemingly a Critic with an axe to grind I should think, as I accidentally ran into him at the COURSE LAUNCH and he was a bad egg!

MIKE looks stunned as if he's channelling MIKE's own thoughts as he distributes assignment sheets.

MIKE

Thanks for the nod of approval THOMAS but that's all retro-speculative, and ancient history now. I've had my time and now it's your time. By the way this sheet-outlines your first assignment: I want a 7-10 minute treatment for a short film in three days' time. I'll take pitches from what I think look to have most potential and when that's done, you as a film team or crew will be apportioned roles picked out of a hat and will then hone them and then shoot and post produce the three ten minute short features films and write and produce a full Pilot for entry in the Academy run FILM festival in 19 weeks' time: And Time is now your enemy. OK back to introductions …how about you start us off BERNADETTE.

The class visibly assess him as now being a reluctant lecturer.

BERNADETTE (EARNEST AND SHY)

Um, I'm Bernadette, erm BERNIE, BERNIE HAWKINS.. I'm almost 21 and hail from agricultural country GABBENGUBBA NSW. I grew up on a farm - you know mixed crops, dairy cows, poultry and pigs! I love pigs because they're so smart and funny and taught me to stop eating bacon and pork. Um, so I guess you could say I know how to crutch sheep, deliver inverted calves, skin a rabbit with my hands, tame a wild brumby.. er, horse, and blow the head off a King Brown snake or Taipan with a 303 at 40 metres.

JUSTIN finds her strangely fascinating. GONERIL has a sneering look and whispers to JUSTIN, sitting next to her..

GONERIL

A regular ANNIE freakin' OAKLEY!

JUSTIN (WHISPERING BACK TO HER)

Why don't you grow some decency and let her tell her story

GONERIL

Why don't you grow a sense of humour, JOCKSTRAP, and blow it out your ass?

JUSTIN is stunned and doesn't know what to make of her

BERNADETTE

I always loved going to the, movies with my family. But I'm not exactly an avid reader

MIKE

Then it's high time you made a start. Make it today! You have to pass Script-writing in this course as well, and you can't write if you don't read. And remember what ROBERT MC KEE said: not Even ROBERT DE NIRO, HELEN MIRREN or RAPH FIENNES as a cast can save a BAD SCRIPT. And not even an OSCAR winning DIRECTORS like STEVEN SPIELBERG or ANG LEE could Direct 120 blank pages. WRITERS create the mind, heart and map of the film, and the GPS system for the DIRECTOR, CINEMATOGRAPHER AND PRODUCTION team to make it happen and finesse it

He selects 5 books from his shelf and hands them to her

Okay, start with "Great Expectations", "Catch 22", "EMMA", MIDDLEMARCH, PARADISE LOST and "THE FEMALE EUNUCH" and the Screenplay "CHINATOWN". These will get you started. And I suggest you start immediately! That goes for anyone else here who doesn't read "Much" as well. Your first texts by the way are in the pile on the table yonder - "Story", "Save the Cat" and STANISLAVSKY

BERNADETTE (NODDING ASSENT)

And I really want to direct. And make films like "An Affair to Remember", "SLEEPLESS in SEATTLE", "Love Actually" and MY BEST FRIEND'S WEDDING". I adore Romantic Comedies"
-MERRIMAN sees snatches of several films she mentions as he "mentally projects them" onto the seminar room's screen and he alternately watches and listens to her and sees (along with the VIEWERS) the images of BURT LANCASTER and DEBORAH

KERR and then TOM HANKS and MEG RYAN.

JULIE (INTERJECTING)

They call them ROMCOMS in Industry parlance.

She's not easy to like.

BERNADETTE

And I want marriage and kids when I finish the degree.. and sooner rather than later..She's a one off. The other STUDENTS look at her almost pityingly, though JUSTIN gives her a philosophical look and BUI HUONG looks compassionate. But GONERIL pretends to stick her finger down her throat. Vulnerable BERNIE is crestfallen and shuts up immediately..

MIKE (EYEBALLING GONERIL)

Let's get one thing clear right from the "Opening Credits": to genuinely succeed in this course you will ALL have to become a proper TEAM. Toleration of each other's personalities, individual interests and exactly who EACH OF YOU is, is absolutely vital. No more of that stuff here...okay?

He reads their name tags and his roll again.

MIKE

So, erm, GONERIL, your Dad is a fan of SHAKESPEARE'S tragedies I gather.

MERRIMAN (WHISPERS TO SANDERS)

GONERIL and REGAN were the two evil daughters of KING LEAR. Though he DID have a loving daughter named CORDELIA..

SANDERS is taken aback believing THOMAS thinks him uneducated.

> **GONERIL (OVERHEARING)**
> Maybe those TWO FEISTY SISTERS in KING LEAR were just misunderstood. But I admit my PAPA wasn't "blind to Irony", and given he never won the Father of the Year Award himself, and I'm the black sheep of the family, maybe he did have a sense of humour after all. Okay, me and then - HIM

She glances dismissively at JUSTIN

> My favourite film is probably "The original EXORCIST" : as an aspiring Actress myself, I thought LINDA BLAIR was a real head turner. And of course the BLAIR WITCH PROJECT was also amusing. One of my long term aims is to make a Musical version of THAT ANCIENT VAMPIRE NOSFERATU starring DAVID SPADE, LADY GAGA, RICKY GERVAIS and SHAQ O'NEILL..

She gives JUSTIN a malevolent grin which he returns. The other MALES are also little wary of her, with the exception of MERRIMAN.

> **JUSTIN (WHISPERING TO MERRIMAN)**
> Does the name GONERIL sound like a social disease to you too?

He's flummoxed. MIKE and JENN see they have some work to do withGONERIL. MERRIMAN now magically "projects" short moving images from the old movie NOSFERTU onto the screen. The spiritually-attuned GONERIL and WALLY HARROWER glance at the screen as he does so almost sensing something is there.

JUSTIN

My favourite films are older ones: I like "THE 39 STEPS and BOBBY BENSON in "ONE ON ONE", the best Basketball feature film ever made. I guess you maybe know I've been a pro football player but now I've said arrivederci to all that. I want to make a film about Rites of Passage and the trials of Adolescence. I'm inspired by "CATCHER IN THE RYE", "Stand By Me" and DENNIS QUAID's great first film, "BREAKING AWAY"

GONERIL smirks so as he sees it. JUSTIN looks deflated by this. .

Whatever.! Ohr yeah, and I also liked that dark short film BAMBI MEETS GODZILLA.

GONERIL

You really are a "Jockular young Strap-ling": aren't you TIGER?

JUSTIN hasn't a clue how to deal with her

BUI HONG

I like BEACHES. And "The Way We Were"."

JULIE (HAUGHTY)

"Fellini and JULIET OF THE SPIRITS" and "CINEMA PARADISO" float my boat. All but MERRIMAN and SANDERS look at her with "What the? Looks, as if she's pretentious.

GONERIL (MUTTERING QUIETLY)

Yeah, her boat being the S.S. MINNOW!

Only MERRIMAN hears her and is fascinated by her truculence.

SANDERS (INGRATIATING)

Absolutely! Yes the Italian directors are often compelling. WALLY, WOLFGANG and SONNY grin at each other over SANDERS' fawning interest in JULIE. MIKE looks to the reluctant MERRIMAN but fails to draw him out. He looks about to have a panic attack till he puts on his Groucho Marx glove puppet,

MIKE

And you, Mr HARROWER...WALLY?

WALLY

"BLOOD SIMPLE AND THE TEXAS CHAINSAW MASSACRE are my cuppa Joe. And "THE CHANT OF JIMMY BLACKSMITH rocked.

MICK, JULIE and MERRIMAN obviously know the KENNEALLY novel and the film of it, and they look at him askance.

MIKE (TO THE OTHERS)

That was an excellent but disturbing FRED SCHEPISI film about Race hate and revenge. Care to elaborate THOMAS?

He's trying to build shy MERRIMAN'S confidence.

MERRIMAN

Erm, it's based on a true story about an ABORIGINAL stockman who went on a chilling murder rampage killing white people at the turn of the 19th century..

GONERIL (INTERJECTING)

Many of our own indigenous people, like the CHEYENNE for example, called that "defending Tribal Lands, or Kicking WHITEY's ass". LITTLE BIG HORN for example...

MIKE

Nice seguey GONERIL...but is there anything you might need to tell us about yourself before we start this course MR HARROWER? No history of psychiatric episodes? Do we need to take out life insurance policies by any chance?

MIKE's ironic because he and JENN can both see the glint in WALLY's eye. He's a good actor and when WALLY moves his Stanislavsky acting book slightly on the table MIKE and MERRIMAN know he's playing a METHOD ROLE for now - the Angry Young "out there" BLACK MAN With a chip on his shoulder. WALLY, MICK AND MERRIMAN have each other's measure now. The other STUDENTS though are wary of both WALLY and GONERIL for the moment.

WALLY (GRINNING SLYLY)

I also really like Frank CAPRA'S' classic "IT'S A WONDERFUL LIFE. You see, growing up in a slum in a dead end Outback N.S.W SLUM TOWN I got a vicarious pleasure from watching middle-class white families living the high life.. You know: Roast chicken...AN OVEN to cook it in, table cloths and family dinners at a clean table, soap, hot showers, clean sheets, watching a TV that works around a warm fire AND NO RATS! Or having to sleep the kennels with the dogs to avoid a drunken beating or...

His "audience" stare in shock. JEN smiles to self.

MIKE

It says here on your student profile your MUM was a VET but died from cancer and your DAD was a Doctor, and that you grew up in one of the most prestigioussuburbs in Sydney, and attended TRINITY GRAMMAR, one of the best and most expensive private Schools in Australia,

Some of the others look at him suspiciously and others start to smirk .

WALLY

That's just some B.S I made up to try to get Into this genetically-selective course.

MIKE and JENN recognize he has some acting chutzpah. Most of the others now know WALLY's been playing the race card for a long time.

JENN

How about You MOSHE

SONNY (MOSHE)

My friends call me SONNY.. I'm a composer and but I want to act as well. My top films were Rodney Dangerfield's "Back to School" and the THREE AMIGOS". I prefer Comedies. And Groucho Marx and the three Stooges of course.

AMAL (SHAKES HIS HAND)

So do I. I want to make comedies like those as well.. Im a MOSLEM girl from TEHERAN and ABU DHABI.

SONNY

Shi iiite!

AMAL (SHE LIKES HIM)

CORRECTAMUNDO but it's a silent T! Do you realize if we formed a comedy DUO.. or a singing DUO – we could call ourselves SUNNI AND SHIA….(LAUGHS)

JENN

So, STEPHANIE RHODES, what's your STORY?

STEPHANIE (DROLL?)

Apparently all TOADS try for RHODES.. I got so sick of kissing frogs I thought maybe I might just find a decent tadpole or MR Semi RIGHT, DOWNUNDER. I grew up in a small town on PRINCE EDWARD ISLAND which really does look just as it does in ANNE OF GREEN GABLES, if you were wondering.Um, I was a straight A student, but wanted to be a VET. Blah, blah!.so I was discovered by an Agent watching me - in a lacrosse game! CREEPY eh? As soon as I finished school, I found myself on the catwalk in CHICAGO and NEW YORK. BIG MONEY but shallow lifestyle, and blah blah. So, I always liked the stage, read about this course, and here I am. That's all she wrote! Oh, and the only acting I've done so far was in the tasteful little Los Angeles PORN flicks TIPHANY'S TANTILIZING TITTIES and PUSSY IN BOOTS. I did them to get over my previous shyness and stage fright…

She laughs and gives SANDERS a sultry look he can't ignore. MIKE and all of the STUDENTS suddenly look at her quite differently.

WOLFGANG

So how did that work out for you TITTYFANNY?

Silence descends. She's gob smacked.

MERRIMAN (WEARING HIS SOCK PUPPET)

I like comedies - especially classic BRITISH films. I think that 50's comic NORMAN WISDOM was a hoot - and Peter Sellers was great in "BEING THERE"…of course,GROUNDHOG DAY was fantasmagorical.

His mind "projects" old footage of W.C Fields then NORMAN WISDOM onto the screen. While no one else sees WISDOM laughing so hard he's wheezing, the strangely spiritual WALLY almost does. The others stare at a blank screen and then at MERRIMAN as if he's certifiable, but then also they too catch his infectious laughter and join in and when he farts because of the laughter it makes them laugh harder. Even GONERIL almost smiles for the first time. He's potentially a health tonic for this lot.

MIKE

You're going have to hang loose for a minute, JENN and I have to speak to DORIAN for a few minutes.

PAN TO:
The students wait on MIKE, JENN and DORIAN somewhat impatiently. Some of them are in conversations, some reading notes or writing.
BUI HUONG secretly watches BRYCE SLOANE in the adjacent Studio as he checks out one of the movie cameras. He sees her looking at him and winks, unseen by the others. She turns away coyly to listen to SANDERS and BERNADETTE's discussion but turns once more to smile at him encouragingly.

BERNADETTE

So you're seriously going to cut all of the Camera skills classes tomorrow on only our second day? I know we have the morning free for a writing assignment but to blow off the full afternoon: Just to do a day's SUBSTITUTE Teaching!.

SANDERS

 Not just any day's teaching though!
MIKE knows I need every $300 cheque I can get my hands on. My Band's weekend gigs barely pay for this course, so tomorrow I actually have to take a Junior High class to the Australian War Memorial in the National Capital National an all day excursion. We fly VIRGIN at 6 A.M and return at 5 PM Somehow I also have to find time to read up on the History of Cinema Detectives for DORIAN's night class as well. I have a DOCTOR mate though and I reckon he'll write me a sick certificate for a drinkable bottle of Beaujolais.

STEPHANIE is clearly interested in SANDERS but he's too interested in JULIE to properly notice and is stressed out by his finance woes. BUI HUONG turns and talks to JULIE, who's trying to overhear the conversation as well. She's had no interest in SANDERS till she saw STEPHANIE's interest. She also notes WOLFGANG fancies STEPHANIE. and her face says: "this is the kind of plot I can rewrite and direct". SANDERS' Dilemma shows she's clearly plotting something.

SCENE.INT. EXT. FILM ACADEMY RECORDING STUDIO. DAY

From the POV of a cleaner buffing the floors and looking through the window into the technical production rooms MIKE is demonstrating the use of the boom, sound recording equipment and the Red Camera, both hand held and on tripods, and showing the students framing techniques. As usual, MERRIMAN provides the non-verbal running commentary explanation for what's happening through bubbles above his head that name focus, lenses, zooming and wide angle, boom and the like.

SCENE.INT.CITY CLUB DANCE.NIGHT

That night WOLFGANG, MERRIMAN and four of the FEMALE STUDENTS take a smaller camera to a dance with a widely disparate group of hopeful romantics and all are seemingly desperately looking for romance with anyone with a pulse. WOLFGANG wants MERRIMAN to provide the dance music on his SOUND AND MUSIC MACHINE .JULIE and STEPHANIE are dressed alluringly and play up to several worn out looking males who are old enough to be their GRANDFATHERS.

WOLFGANG

Okay THOMAS can I try your machine. I've got an Idea how to liven up these GUYS' night.

He turns off the Forties Band Music and plays around with the dials on MERRIMAN'S machine. Suddenly a medley of fast booming Rock and Roll dance songs start playing. The old MEN try to impress their young dance partners by dancing to it. They last about a minute. STEPHANIE angrily turns it off. The OLDIES look like they could have heart attacks.

STEPHANIE

What an A List Nob! Do you actually possess one ounce of sensitivity, you Teutonic oaf! That could've killed someone!

She storms off and the young WOMEN sit down at tables with the

OLD MEN to chat and check none of them keels over. WOLFIE looks dumbfounded. No one it seems, has ever talked to him that way. He walks out with MERRIMAN, and truly seems to reflect on her words..

SC. INT.STUDENT APARTMENTS LOUNGE AND RECREATION AREA

Everyone's hanging out in the mess area. It's late and MERRIMAN watches GONERIL as he drifts off into dreamland, smitten. He projects his SURREAL BUT SEEMINGLY REALISTIC DREAM onto the large LED TV screen in the RECREATION ROOM. In a moment the images DISSOLVE to old B&W and FILM NOIR. In his daydream GONERIL's, dressed in 1930's fashion clothes and with her hair in a bun resembles an American femme fatale of that era. She gets out of a classic automobile and climbs the stairs to the first story office of THOMAS B MERRIMAN, PRIVATE DETECTIVE. It's just like a SURREAL VIGNETTE from The MALTESE FALCON and when BUI HUONG, dressed as an ASIAN secretary leads her into THOMAS'S office, the interior looks like a facsimile of SAM SPADE's office. There's even a statue of a dodo on his desk that for a split second is reminiscent of the MALTESE FALCON. There's also a TALKING PARROT walking around across MERRIMAN's big desk like he owns the joint. MERRIMAN is dressed in dark pin stripe suit and a fedora and has a matchstick protruding from his teeth. He ushers his sexy TRIBAL looking SECRETARY (BUI HUONG) away with a wave of his hand.

> **THOMAS BUD MERRIMAN P.I (TO GONERIL)**
> Hello DOLL-FACE. You must be MELODY HARTFORD .. of The HAMPTON, HEREFORD or THOMAS BUD MERRIMAN...HIGHFIELD HARTFORDS I'm guessing. I can actually hold a melody you know.

HE HUMS.

THOMAS (CONT.)

So where's the fire? Your phone-call sounded urgent. Do you need the key to our toilet?

MELODY (GONERIL)

N..NO I don't! And YES, it is urgent, MISTER MERRIMAN.

TALKING PARROT

Call me BUD.

BUD MERRIMAN

Ignore him. I'M BUD. It's A PRIVATE INVESTIGATOR M.O, and also my Middle name! It's Short for BUDDINGTON

PARROT

BALONEY! It's short for BUDGERIGAR

MELODY

Who's running this Office?

PARROT & BUD (TOGETHER

I AM!

MELODY

I ..I know this is going to sound crazy.

THOMAS BUD MERRIMAN

Just try me SISTER. I've been round the BLOCK a few times… Y'KNOW what I'm sayin?

MELODY

W..Well...alright then. Um, BUD, do you believe in ALIENS.The PARROT craps on the table. BUD writes on his note pad: "FRUITLOOP?"

THOMAS BUD MERRIMAN

We talking illegal ALIENS

His tribal ASIAN SECRETARY suddenly falls into the room while eavesdropping at the door.

Or legal ALIENS? Keep goin' LADY. I charge by the hour though.

MELODY

I'm talking about Extra-Terrestrial ALIENS. I'm a GGod-fearing woman M..Mister M MERRIMAN, erm, BUD and I swear on the HOLY BIBLE.. I was..I was..

PARROT

That's a bummer of a stutter you got there Lady.

MELODY

I was abducted from my family home two weeks ago by two swarthy metre high ALIENS who ...who..

PARROT

I also speak OWL fluently, so..THOMAS almost falls out of his chair straining to hear something salacious as his eyes fight not to wander over her body. Suddenly there's a crash and a flash as the images return to colour and THOMAS falls out of his chair and back in the real world of the STUDENT LOUNGE. He's prostrate and looking up at GONERIL, humiliated, as she screws up her eyes and mouth at him, and almost grins. A second time!.

WOLFGANG (LAUGHING)

Take it easy there THOMAS. Daydreaming can be a dangerous pastime.

SCENE. SEMINAR ROOM.DAY

The room is darkened and the projector prepped for Screening, when the class enter the room.

MIKE

Seeing you all have to make several films by mid December I thought I'd show you a recent one I made. It's a true story about my younger brother BILLY when he was 13. I showed it at his funeral a a few days ago and it's call,,,

The class mood changes suddenly to respectful and intense.

... A SMALL MATTER OF HONOUR

SCENE.INT.EXT.SHEARING -SHED.NEW ENGLAND.DAY (POSSIBLE ANIMATION?)

ALAN (NARRATOR MIKE'S VOICE-OVER)

I was shearing with JOHNNO JOHNSON's gang in the New England area, to the north of TAMWORTH It was my third season with JOHNNO's gang but most of the rest of them had been together, through the shearing season for eight or ten years.

The visuals show a few shearers coming and going from the shed and sheep milling around in a holding pen nearby. In the background is a homestead with a veranda and two four wheel drives parked outside. The smoky and pristine hills of New England define the horizon.
The POV flits from one to another as they go about their tasks... briefly following one as he fixes his shearing gear, another who sweeps out shed and another who brings some billy tea, cups and

biscuits. Another listens to a transistor radio and yet another pens a letter.

MIKE/ALAN (NARRATOR)

> There were seven of us in the gang and we worked four months or so each year, starting in mid-August and going through into December. When the season ended we'd all go back to fruit-picking, or digging spuds or whatever everyone did with the rest of the year. Shearing's hard work and when you finish for the day all you want is a bite to eat, a couple of beers and your bed. So there's neither the time nor the inclination to get involved with the locals except maybe to say G'day if you see them. We just mind our own affairs and they mind theirs. And time is money for us so, while the work is there, we get stuck into it and that's that - except if it's raining and the wool is wet or if we're travelling between jobs - we work seven days a week from dawn to dusk. We live together, eat together and drink together. I guess you could say the shearing gang becomes a tight little family that thinks and acts as one. Question, of course, is 'One what'?

The POV swings wide again and pans across the veranda and house and across the expansive property. A lone horsewoman canters across the flatlands through herds of sheep towards the shearers, a kelpie trotting alongside.

MIKE

> Anyway, we hit this property in September. It was a good station of a few thousand acres of real nice sheep country. The place was owned and run by a middle-aged widow,

SCENE.EXT. HOMESTEAD NEAR SHEARERS' QUARTERS. DAY

Alan, hard faced gun shearer watches her ride up to them. He pats the mare as she reigns it in

ALAN

Gidday Mrs MC CABE. We're all rarin' t start tomorrer mornin.

MRS MARY MC CABE (60, FIT)

Good to hear it ALANA. It'd be good for the wool sales if you'd finish within nine days..even ten would be fine.

ALAN (NODDING)

Long as the weather holds.

They look up at a slightly cloudy sky.

MRS MC CABE

I meant to ask how my nephews are going. I'm sorry to land them on you but it's school holidays for another week and it's helping out my sister, so it's appreciated.

They both look towards the shearers' quarters where a solid boy of 15 (MITCH) and his younger but equally tough looking brother Glen (14) are playing French cricket and throwing the tennis ball hard at each other.

ALAN

No probs there Missus. MITCH and GLEN are good value country kids. They're from Walgett, in the Bush yeah.

> **MRS MC CABE (NODS)**
> Oh, and there's another one coming. City kid named BILLY. The son of an old..boyfriend...

His look shows his surprise at this news.

> BILLY's a bit younger and greener than these two. I hope you don't mind?

He shrugs. City KIDS don't seem too welcome with these blokes.
DISSOLVE TO

SCENE.INT.SHEARING SHED.DAY

The pace is full on inside the shed. The shearers are hard at it and the sheep are being herded in by the brothers. It's a hive of activity.

SCENE.EXT.TAMWORTH AIRPORT.DAY.

Mrs MC CABE and a wiry youth of 13 walk towards an old Holden Ute.

SCENE EXT. COUNTRYSIDE BETWEEN TAMWORTH AND BARRABA.DAY

BILLY's a wiry youth with hair in the longer style of early seventies rock musicians and his clothes erring a little on the trendy side. He watches the passing countryside happily and seems up for adventure.

> **MRS MC CABE**
> You ever ridden a horse before son. How'd you like to come with me on a seven mile sheep muster?

He shakes his head but his face says he wants to have a go.

SCENE.EXT.MC CABE SHEEP STATION.DAY

The vision matches the NARRATOR's voice

NARRATOR MIKE

Like typical country kids the brothers could ride, drive a tractor, round up cattle, chop the wood, and do anything else that needed doing. They knew how a shearing shed was run and they made themselves useful. After work, when they weren't larking about or swimming at the damn, they'd be around the shearers' quarters listening to the yarns that were told with the evening beer. One day the pair of them would be running properties of their own if their father had enough money and, if not, they would be managing places for someone else. We all liked them.

SCENE EXT.SHEEP STATION.DAY

The Ute passes baked fields and wheat fields and turns of the empty country road into a long dirt drive heading towards the National Heritage looking homestead. BILLY opens the big gate and locks it after she drives over the cattle grate.
The Ute pulls in next to the steps up to the stylish shady veranda and MITCH and GLEN are standing waiting.
They greet Mrs Mc CABE enthusiastically but as BILLY struggles out with a heavy duffel bag and grins at them in a friendly way, both brothers take an instant dislike to him and Geoff's face sags.

MRS MC CABE

MITCH, GLEN..come and meet BILLY. He'll be staying here for a week with us and working with you two in the sheds. I'd like you both to look after him,because he's never been on a farm before - never even been on a horse either. I'm counting on you boys...okay?

They give her a grudging nod and head off for the sheds.

SCENE.EXT.INT.STABLES.DAY

Mrs MC CABE leads a horse from the stable towards BILLY.

MRS MC CABE

His name's CHESTER and he's yours till you head home next week. Take that saddle over there and have some practice with him.

BILLY's face lights up as he pats the beautiful animal. It's like something essential missing from him has materialized as if by magic.

SC. INT.EXT. SHEARING SHED AND SHEEP YARD. DAY

Inside the sheds it's a frantic pace as the shearers are hard at it and the three boys are working hard sweeping and collecting the fleeces and stacking them and refilling water mugs for the thirsty sweaty shearers.
As BILLY hurries towards the wool tables GLEN sticks out his foot and the younger boy topples over, as MITCH and GLEN and a couple of shearers laugh loudly. These shearers, like the brothers, don't like this city kid either, but at least the boys have the excuse of youthful ignorance..
BILLY gets up and dusts down his clothes. He struggles against the humiliation and hurt as he sees them all laugh at him and cannot understand their nastiness.

MITCH

Sorry about that BELINDA, my foot must've slipped..

BILLY

My name's BILLY...

                               MITCH
    Of course it is - but when your hair's as long as a
    girl's you gotta understand why I mistook you for a
    BELINDA.

The GHOST OF billy watches wistfully at the screen as The BOYS laugh again as do some of the "ugly adult" shearers, who encourage the brothers. BILLY looks at them in despair but then in resignation gets back to carrying the wool. DISSOLVE TO

A series of DISSOLVES show the day's activities and the shorn sheep being shoved out into the yard adjoining the unshorn sheep. SHEARERS look spent, as do the boys as sundown comes.

SCENE.EXT.OUTSIDE THE BUNKHOUSE. SUNDOWN.

They all sit around on chairs or the stoop drinking cups of tea and eating sandwiches. The brothers are popular with the shearers but BILLY sits alone and is clearly ostracized by all.

SCENE.EXT STABLES.SUNDOWN.

BILLY saddles CHESTER and mounts efficiently but has trouble getting him to canter. The BROTHERS have secretly creep up behind them and MITCH throws a large lit cracker towards the horse. It explodes and CHESTER gallops off into the gloaming. BILLY clings desperately to its mane. The BROTHERS crack up, not realizing Mrs MC CABE is watching. She runs to the stables and gallops after the fleeing horse.

SCENE.EXT.MC CABE SHEEP STATION DUSK.

She manages to catch him after almost a mile.

MRS MC CABE

Wow! Amazing! You managed to stay on CHESTER at full gallop yet tell me you've never even been on a horse before?

BILLY'S ashen-faced

> Don't worry son, I'll deal with the BROTHERS.But I can assure you it's really not like them to do something awful like that though

BILLY

Please don't say anything to them. I'll be alright.

She studies him curiously as they walk the horses back. DISSOLVE TO:

SCENE.INT.SHEARING SHED. MORNING

In the morning everyone is hard at it. BILLYs on his game now and stays well clear of the brothers.
In the afternoon there's a heavy rain and the SHEARERS and BROTHERS sit around drinking tea till the unshorn sheep dry out. Without warning GLEN creeps up behind BILLY and grabs him round the waste holding his arms and MITCH arrives with some shears and clips off a big lump of BILLY's hair and they and a few of the SHEARERS think it a great joke as GLEN releases him. BILLY stands there for a few seconds glaring at the brothers and at WAYMAN (25, lean and vulpine), the nastiest SHEARER, and BILLY'S face goes white with rage.

BILLY (TO THE BROTHERS)

That's it! Outside now! You inbred country gonads...

The brothers are disbelieving but smirk at each other as they head towards the exit to the corral area. The bored SHEARERS think this great and several of them chant in unison "Fight! Fight"! One of them though is unimpressed by his work mates and shakes his head at them.

SCENE.EXT. CORRALL AREA.MORNING

There's a break in the rain as they all tramp down the ramp, with the three boys in front. There's only the yard of trampled dirt with no grass. A few sheep mill about in a pen in one corner. The SHEARERS lounge back against the fence rails and light their roll your own cigarettes.

WAYMAN

Come on, Have a go! Have a go BELINDA.

BILLY glances at WAYMAN with cold fury and steals himself. He hauls off his jumper and rolls up his sleeves to show skinny arms. MITCH looks him over and smirks again.

MITCH

I'm not going to fight you, BELINDA. You're too piss-weak for me. GLEN can have you.

GLEN grins cockily and throws his jumper to JOHNNO. He steps forward and squares off. In a moment they were at it, hammer and tongs, GLEN has the reach and is fitter and heavier than BILLY. The gang looks like they expect the fight to last about half a minute and give GLEN noisy encouragement.
But BILLYs a surprise packet: when GLEN gives an inch he steps forward. GLEN shows self-doubt and WAYMAN and a few others stop barracking. Suddenly GLEN goes down and BILLY leaps onto his chest and hits him hard with his knobbly fists. GLEN covers his head and BILLY now gets off him and stands up. No one says a word.

BILLY (TO MITCH)

Now you,

The SHEARERS are silent and the smoke from their cigarettes circle up lazily in the still morning air.

MITCH

I'm four inches taller than you, BELINDA!

BILLY punches him on the mouth and then they go at it. MITCH is older, bigger, and stronger and gives the smaller boy a lacing. The only sound is the shuffle of feet and the thud of fist on flesh and the laboured noise of breathing. The dust from the sheep droppings hangs over them like a grey cloud. When BILLY gets knocked down for the third time, the COOK speaks out

COOKIE

That's enough. We'll call it all square"

JOHNNO (LEAD SHEARER)

Had enough, kid?

BILLY shakes his head and gets up again. There's blood on his face and his shirt's mostly ripped off but he never takes a step backwards and he never stops fighting. In the end MITCH is exhausted and flops down onto the sheep dirt.

MITCH

I've had enough. You've got guts kid..er., BILLY. I'm sorry about using the sheers and for giving you a rough time..

The MEN stand around looking embarrassed. BILLY glares at WAYMAN and takes a step towards him.

BILLY (SHAKING IN FEAR AND ANGER)

You're much worse than them! You're a grown MAN but you keep calling me a girl's name. I'm not afraid of you, either..

Despite being in his mid-twenties WAYMAN is about to "go" for the BOY till the GUN SHEARER steps between them with clenched fists.

JOHNNO

You gutless wanker, WAYMAN! Don't bloody-well show your face around here again for at least 24 hours. Fuck off!

WAYMAN cowers from him and then skulks off towards an old HOLDEN Utility parked near the Shearers' Quarters.

SCENE.EXT.CORRALL NEAR SHEARING SHEDS.

Suddenly Mrs MC CABE walks from an adjacent building. She's seen the whole incident. She hands BILLY his jumper and. JOHNNO nods at him in approval for what he has done..

JOHNNO

Hey, hold on a minute."

BILLY turns towards him but there's no expression on his face.

I'm saying sorry to you, WILL, erm, BILLY, from all of us. You've got more guts than anyone I know and I reckon we all owe you an apology."

Shamefaced, the other shearers follow suit. MITCH and GLEN shake his hand and BILLY softens and is pleased when they knicknamed him 'WILL'.

SCENE.EXT GULLY AND RIVER NEAR ON THE SHEEP STATION.DAY

BILLY and the brothers all skylark on horseback in a picturesque ravine then ride back and tether the horses.

GLEN

> MRS MC CABE gave WAYMEN his marching orders and he has to leave by midday. I had an idea for his going away present. Something wrapped in leather!

MITCH and BILLY watch GLEN sneak onto the veranda with a sizable turd he's just produced. Outside WAYMAN'S small room he grabs ONE of the shearer's riding boots and neatly slides in the poo banana into it the boot and replaces it. The boys then hide out of sight. A Minute later all Hell breaks loose when WAYMAN pulls on the offending boot

WAYMAN (YELLING AND HOWLING)

> I'll kill the bastard who done this…I'll end 'im!

Right then JOHNNO brings out WAYMAN'S suitcase and demands the unit key. The three BOYS're still laughing as WAYMAN drives off in fury.

MIKE (VISION MATCHES NARRATION)

> The boys were good mates after that. BILLY - was just the same as before. There was a difference though. It was in us SHEARERS. We all knew we hadn't given the KID a fair go and we knew he'd proved himself a better man than any of us. It's funny but that was the last year that particular GANG was together. Everyone seemed to wander away and join other shearing teams. Neither JOHNNO nor I even finished the season.

THE END

SCENE.EXT/INT NATIONAL WAR MEMORIAL PACIFIC EXHIBIT DAY

From the POV of increasingly casual VIETNAMESE bodyguard MINH, Bui HUONG and JULIE can be seen entering the main gallery of the WAR MUSEUM. BUI HUONG hasn't a clue he's shadowing her. DISSOLVE

..INT.WAR MEMORIAL CANBERRA.PACIFIC WAR EXHIBITION.DAY.

JULIE AND BUI HUONG have followed him there. They wander the galleries and study the portraits of young men long dead. They stop and examine a painting of a pitched battle in the SOLOMAN ISLANDS.

> **JULIE:**
> Wars have got to be the dumbest things human beings ever conceived. Funny thing too, the ones who start them seldom fight them and it's always men who start them.

> **BUI HUONG:**
> What about PRIME MINISTER MARGARET THATCHER? She started the Falklands War in 1981!

> **JULIE:**
> You're not hearing me: I said WOMEN don't start wars."

BUI HUONG shakes her head. JULIE's a terrible cynic.

> **BUI HUONG:**
> But that must be for reason that not so many WOMEN have power.

JULIE grunts. She'll never be convinced. DISSOLVE TO:

INT. ANOTHER GALLERY FEATURING THE PACIFIC THEATRE.
When they arrive at a PACIFIC WAR DIORAMA exhibit featuring jungle- fighting between Americans, AUSTRALIANS AND JAPANESE they find SANDERS addressing a CLASS of 12 year-old STUDENTS.
CRANE POV TO ZOOM:
STEVE SANDERS sees them and looks shocked, then angry and thenpanicky and way out of his comfort zone completely as these kids are smart and inquisitive. JULIE at first looks judgemental of his ignorance of the subject he's teaching and then she has to fight to suppress laughter at the situation.
He reads a document aloud but just within "earshot" of the disinterested students and stops periodically to give half-informed comments about the exhibit. He suddenly looks increasingly embarrassed and keeps clearing his throat and glancing at JULIE to see if she is laughing at him.

BUI HUONG
Now I wish I had not told you he was teaching here today. You are making him lose face.

SANDERS
And um, er, the JAPANESE Army were much um, better erm, stronger than everyone thought and they were pretty good jungle fighters.

He locks eyes with JULIE's over the kids' heads as he speaks. She gives him the thumbs up sign with a mischievous grin on her face. Sanders has gone bright red but JULIE is merciless and will not walk away

TOBY: (12, A SHARP, SMART STIRRER)

MISTER SANDERS? When did this happen Mister Sanders?

SANDERS:

Um …1940 erm……? He looks at JULIE for confirmation but

JULIE shakes her head at him. She holds up two fingers and he changes his mind on the date.
　　I mean 1942 of course.

Again she gives him the thumbs up

SANDERS

The war with JAPAN began after their sneak attack on Pearl Harbour against the U.S Pacific Fleet

Once more he looks at Julie, who is now nodding enthusiastically

TOBY:

But why did the JAPANESE want to kill AMERICAN and AUSTRALIAN people?"SANDERS has a 3 second animated racist thought bubble of lusty Japanese soldiers chasing attractive Aussie women down a street. He starts to panic as he flicks through his notes. In desperation he looks at at JULIE and while she looks sympathetic, she won't leave.

SANDERS (BROW WRINKLING)

Well …erm, they resented America…

He awaits her ongoing clever mimes telling him what to say

SANDERS

Because …American was a rich country partly in the Pacific... and Japan um

JULIE mouths "Needed more land and saw America as a threat"

Wanted more land and the Japanese thought if … they could occupy some huge Pacific territory quickly then……."

TOBY turns for a second and just catches part of JULIE's clever mime.

TOBY: (FIENDISHLY)

Are you a History teacher MR SANDERS?"JULIE puts her hand over her mouth, and her eyes water.

SANDERS:

Well, no…erm…
He reads the kid's name from his list.
TOBY, not as such! I'm erm, a Musician and I'm also an Actor actually.

TOBY:

Ohhh! You're a substitute teacher then!

Suddenly all the kids in the group give each other knowing looks as the penny drops. SENDERS knows
he has lost them, so he distributes work sheets that correspond to the exhibitions

SANDERS:

Okay everyone that's enough of the forty questions and character assassination! Now I want you all to work through these research sheets in this gallery and in the one up the stairs over there and report back to me here in an hour with everything completed. Got that? That's 2.30 in Real Time. Now make like LEPRECHAUNS and disappear!"

They disperse to different exhibits laughing and babbling as they go. SANDERS looks at JULIE AND BUI HUONG, totally frazzled.

JULIE:

Did you ever wonder if you were in the right profession MR SANDERS?

He walks over to them with a peeved look.

SANDERS

I CANNOT BELIEVE YOU!! YOU FAIR DINKUM

Caught a bloody plane and followed me here? To humiliate me, right? So JULIE, it seems you're something of a SADIST.

BUI HUONG looks up the word "" in her special dictionary.

JULIE:

And that would make you a MASOCHIST. We're flying back in an hour. I treated BUI HUONG to a trip. I've got scholarship money at the moment. So, are you really a MUSICIAN? I bet you're in a Covers Band.

SANDERS

We play pretty much everything - including our own material. Have you heard of the WEAPING WIZARDS?

JULIE

Pronounced like Orphan ANNIE saying Leaping Lizards? Yeah, I've heard them on the Radio. That's pretty good."

SANDERS:

I'm only doing weekend gigs with them now till I finish the UNI course.

JULIE

But SUBSTITUTE Teaching: You!

SANDERS

Hell I don't know. The movie course is eating my finances. They were desperate for a teacher. Obviously! I like kids but fact is I can't really cut the mustard. You've apparently realized, I've never studied history – except as a SCHOOLKID. In this job though they can give you any old subject. Tough on you and tougher on the poor little bastards you teach.

BUI HUONG picks up on the chemistry between them and wanders over to a painting of a CORAL SEA battle and leaves them alone. For a second she glimpses a VIETNAMESE man who seems to be looking at her but she blinks AND he's gone. She's not sure if she saw anything.

SCENE. INT. WORLD WAR EUROPEAN EXHIBITS GALLERY. DAY

TOBY and another pupil spy on their TEACHER and JULIE from behind a bronze statue of a COAST WATCHER IN HIDING and are giggling hysterically.

JULIE: (CONSULTING HER WATCH)

Well, it's certainly been um, interesting.

SANDERS: (IRONICALLY)

I get it. Interesting like in the old CHINESE curse: May you live interesting times.

JULIE:

Bingo! Now you're getting the hang of it. Anyway.... we have to be going. So, my advice is, don't miss any more classes.

SANDERS:

You still haven't answered me. Why?

She half turns and shrugs then keeps walking

I was just thinking. You don't like MEXICAN food by any chance?"

She continues walking but half turns and smiles as she goes.

SANDERS

How about Turkish? Greek? Lebanese
Again she turns as she walks. This time she stops about fifteen metres from him.

JULIE:

I'm a vegetarian.

SANDERS:

Some of my best friends were conceived over tofu and hummus.

JULIE:

This course is full on! And I'm not looking for a relationship.

SANDERS:

I'm not offering one. It's just dinner for God's sake!"

JULIE

Do you ever go to the PARADISE ROCK CLUB in town on a Thursday night?

SANDERS:

Do polar bears love Eskimo pies?

JULIE

Well., might see you there some time. When I'm not doing the course essays..

SANDERS

YOU DO REALIZE We live in the same Apartment complex at the moment, you Loony! We'll see each other every day.

JULIE

Sure, but where the mystery in that? Actors and writers need motivation and intrigue.

BILLY THE GHOST

Just ask me about motivation why don't you?

She gives SANDERS an enigmatic smile and calls out to BUI HUONG, but she thinks she sees someone she recognizes, skulking in a nearby gallery. It's MINH her secret Minder. He and SANDERS separately watch them disappear at the top of the stairs.

SCENE.INT. VIETNAM WAR EXHIBIT GALLERY.DAY
The two PUPILS who were spying on SANDERS saunter up to him grinning like macaques.

> **TOBY:**
>
> Sir? MISTER SANDERS - Do you just take students to places like this so you can meet GIRLS
>
> **SANDERS: (WRY SMILE)**
>
> That's an interesting question TOBY: You ever consider a career as a COP or PRIVATE EYE?

He glances at his watch and then towards the next gallery.

> Now go and round up the others please SHERLOCK. It's time we caught the Bus.
>
> **TOBY:**
>
> It looks like you've already missed it sir.He looks in the direction the young WOMEN just took.
>
> **SANDERS:**
>
> Very funny Mister Clever clogs. Now get moving before I accidentally misplace your assignment: or better yet, swear I never received it.

Teacher and pupil have a good understanding of each other's sense of the ironic and Sanders makes a warlike face at TOBY before the two kids hurry off laughing. DISSOLVE TO:

SCENE.INT.LECTURE THEATRE EDDY KELLY ACADEMY. DAY

The students are waiting for MIKE to arrive for an SF lecture. FROM MERRIMAN'S EYES POV they're each dressed as their favourite SF characters, so there's JULIE as Princess LEIA, MERRIMAN as YODA, JUSTIN as CHEWBACCA, SANDERS as a Bad Robot and so on. MIKE actually does arrive dressed in full DARTH VADER uniform and with the aid of a electronic voice resonating microphone starts off mimicking JAMES EARL JONES' Dark Lord's deep scary voice.

> **MIKE (IN D.VADER CHARACTER AND VOICE)**
> How do fellow Vulcans

He makes Vulcan split fingers sign

> Today's subject is SCIENCE FICTION in films and TV. Basically, we're looking at STORY and PLOT in a scripting and pitching exercise you need to be able to distil a screenplay into a sentence.
> So let's do three minutes' brain storming as a practice exercise. I'll start you off with some titles and you complete tag lines incorporating the essence of the films. Anyone can come in at any time in this game: just a short pithy line getting to the some of the DNA of each of the films I name, okay? Make it funny or witty and May the Schwarz be with you.MIKE projects a computer slide show on a smart board showing a vast number of movie poster images matching the films he names and MERRIMAN switches on his SFX and music system to complement the images so everyone else can hear the sounds now.

MIKE (CHARACTER VOICES)

Unfortunately, with many SF movies today, the viewer often gains a nagging feeling of DEJA VU... DIDN'T I just say that? I mean, it's always the twenty ninth century

MERRIMAN

And I thought MY watch was fast..!

MIKE (NODDING APPROVAL)

Youth is still rebellious, those Scum-bag Gung Ho Out-casters want to take over the planet and vaporize anyone with a MULLET OR pony tail, human essentials such as..

MERRIMAN

MOET French champagne?

MIKE

That's it! And other creature comforts still cost a fistful of ...

JUSTIN

Not dollars, but plastic?

MIKE

Now you've got it: I think you've got it! And there's yet another heretical mystic on the JIHAD horizon, and, to paraphrase WOODY ALLEN, Epsilon girls still prefer.....

STEPHANIE

French kissing to hand-shaking..?

MICK (SMILING)

She's good this one! I also have to agree with
WOODY that what most people
want to know about life in outer space is..

MERRIMAN

..Do they have Ray Guns?"

They're impressed by MERRIMAN too. Even GONERIL is.

SONNY(MOSHE LEVI JUMPING IN)

Film title idea flash: VENUS IN BLUE GENES in
Blue GENES AKA SHEER FOLLY.

MIKE is happy they're "getting with the program. MERRIMAN projects classic SF Films on screen while they respond

MIKE

And according to the Night Manager at my PUB,
which is called the...

SANDERS

The WOOKIE AND CHILD?

This gets a grin from MIKE and smiling approval from STEPHANIE and JULIE, both now in open competition for his attentions, though STEPHANIE leaves him in no doubt he'll of plenty of action if he chooses her.

MIKE

Science Fiction as a genre in film and stories is a
major shape-changer and a shameless plunderer of
everything from myths and magic to high Science
versus Creationism, for instance, led to ripping
yarns like the one about that BIG GOOMBAH,
Frankenstein's monster...

MOSHE -SONNY (APPREHENSIVELY)

..a Man of many parts.

MIKE smiles encouragingly

WOLFGANG

So, how do you, nally, rank the best movie Science Fiction I wonder?

MIKE

Well, identifying some of the best SF on celluloid, um, one such best movie list could comprise the following: "Metropolis" I call it New York without the traffic snarls; Then there's the old Eastern Bloc's SOLARIS or Spaced out Spouse; "The Omega Man".. UM, CHARLTON HESTON's last Swiss watch; "LOGAN's RUN" is about citizens being killed as soon as they reach 30 or so, so you can retitle it not the Bold and the Beautiful, but "The OLD and the Dutiful"; "Village of the Damned" is about Alien children in our midst so it's like maybe "Cuckolds Anonymous; "A for Andromeda" sounds like a B.B.C Dramatization of the alphabet; AND STANLEY KUBRICK'S "2001"..

BERNADETTE

MY MENTOR WOTH A MONOLITH?

JUSTIN

YETH, or 1470 MAN FINDS ATOMIC INSPIRATION BEFORE LUNCH ...

MIKE (NODDING APPROVAL)

And how about RIDLEY SCOTT's "ALIEN"?

JULIE

What about JAWS - ON ACID? He gives her the thumbs up

WALLY

OR "E.T.- a Bell TELEPHONE CO promo spectacular,and "BLADE RUNNER " ..

MERRIMAN

I ROBOT, You JANE"..and "STAR WARS: MERLIN, KING ARTHUR AND MORDRED REINCARNATED IN A GALAXY FAR, FAR AWAY – it's almost a direct steal from the KING ARTHUR stories.

They're somewhat impressed with MERRIMAN and no one can really match him. SLOANE stands unseen near the doorway and watches

MIKE

How about another SF film that could be included in any list - the Close Encounters of the WORST KIND megahit "INDEPENDENCE DAY - I.D. 4". I reckon it can be summarized in a couple of lines as follows: U.F.O's. STOP! N.Y.C, R.S.V.P.STOP!, E.T's. STOP! FBI, CIA - S.N.A.F.U.STOP!.E.T's S.O.B's. STOP! S.O.SI.B.M's F18's. STOP! E.T's D.O.A. STOP! U.N. A.O.K. STOP! OVER AND OUT

He now looks pointedly at SONNY (MOSHE)

SONNY/ MOSHE

OR How about: ISRAELIS and PALESTINIANS vigorously reject Alien WEST BANK solution...

AMAL

SONNY, you ain't no "GENTILE man! Dot's fer shure!

AMAL pretends to bop MOSHE on the head (a la MOE) and SONNY pretends to twist her nose off (A LA CURLEY) while MERRIMAN provides the proper sound effects accompaniment on his machine.

MIKE

This isn't Elementary school GUYS. Any Other takes on INDEPENDENCE DAY?

STEPHANIE (GIVING SANDERS THE EYE)

Why not Inter Galactic Terra-formers Poleaxed by Computer NERD..?

JULIE and STEPHANIE are now official enemies. SANDERS is confused

MOSHE (SONNY)

Or.. "Feisty PRESIDENT kicks arses of ALIENS with Altitude Problem".

MIKE (HE'S PLEASED WITH THEM)

And as for the genetic engineering romp "JURASSIC PARK", basically it as...

BUI HONG (NERVOUSLY)

What DINAH Saw.

Their smiles reassure her. GONERIL visibly thinks a few of her PEERS are showing promising signs of becoming tolerable.

MIKE

We'll start winding up this riffing… Just a couple more: our somewhat more-recent offerings were: "MINORITY REPORT"- Foxy PRECOG gets bad vibe about CRUISE marriage; AND - "SIGNS" ..

MERRIMAN

MEL GIBSON'S "Field of Dreams – bad dreams" : IF YOU BUILD CROP CIRCLES They WILL COME ;

It's almost a double act

MIKE

.And "THE MATRIX"?

JULIE

Hmmmm – how about genius COMPUTER WHIZ Hacks Into Techno Babble and SFX MOTHERLODE.

MIKE grins at her. His approval makes her happy. He seems to get her.

WALLY (RAPPER IMPERSONATION)

Yeah, and fortunately for the movie "I ROBOT", its Director ALEX PROYAS had Studio permission to Edit WIILL SMITH'S Robotophobic "Don't be Dissin me you metal MUTHA or you is gonna be in a world a hurt assembling Bitsaremissin, er MITSUBISHI, automobiles in the Detroit city stain….." to "the first rule of Robotics is that a robot cannot harm a human" – yeah and white pointers are vegetarian! I LOVED THAT MOVIE!

SLOANE looks disdainful until he gets a hot look from BUI HUONG.

MIKE

Why then has some of the best SF, dystopic Literature from the past and present become more relevant today in the form of feature films? Why do "BRAVE NEW WORLD", "1984","DAY OF THE TRIFFIDS", "ALIEN" and horrible realistic stories like "CHILDREN OF MEN get so much attention?

JUSTIN

It's just a feeling, but it seems that despite all the technological breakthroughs and medical advancements we've achieved, that stress free human life and our world is more and more under siege. I think there are just too many people on the planet and individual and collective dangers are growing because of climate change…and

STEPHANIE (NODDING)

Exactly, and famines, PLAGUES, AIDS, ICE epidemics, greed, murderous fanatics and religious militarism, for a start are all symptoms of growing levels of world mental illness.. The growing risk of rogue terrorists using nuclear and chemical weapons scares everybody into a collective fear that feeds on itself.. SF anticipates potential worst case scenarios: I REALLY MISS STEVEN HAWKING being in the world, I have to say, and he and other futurists warn Artificial I intelligence could threaten our existence as well. Dystopic SF is just a fictional response to deep-seated and often justifiable human fears for the future and at best SCIENCE FICTION provides important warnings. At worst it gives the MONSTERS among us, like psychopathic certain LEADERS, even more dangerous ideas.

WOLFGANG notices her passion as well as her beauty. Most of them there seem to agree with her. MERRIMAN accidentally pushes the wrong switch and they all hear the music from the Twilight Zone and Alzo Sprach Zarathustra and the others turn to look at him. He suddenly notices GONERIL seems strangely nervy and harassed and HE shudders as a bipedal lizard-like ALIEN on each side of her starts to come into focus. He sees they're nasty and fanged little boogers pinch her and whisper gutteral sounds in her ears.

MERRIMAN suddenly LEAPS from his chair and rushes round behind GONERIL with two water jugs from the table and just as the Aliens turn to see him he empties the jugs over them. Their high pitched screams are inaudible to everyone but MERRIMAN and GONERIL. The others all gape at him but he ignores them and whacks the Aliens with a chair and watches in awe as they dissolve squealing..

MERRIMAN

Well it worked for MEL GIBSON's character in SIGNS and also for the Wicked Witch of the West, and also worked with these weevils!

GONERIL looks up at him and appears to be coming out of some part trance. She suddenly realizes what he has done and stands and hugs him caringly, fighting tears. They now sit as if almost nothing has happened and wait for MIKE to finish the lecture. GONERIL is a different person. The rest of the group and a now-animated-SLOANE, goggle at them, stunned.

MIKE

For Christ's sake THOMAS! Clean that up! What the Hell WAS that?

SLOANE now stands at the back and walks to the front

> **SLOANE**
>
> Okay. I've seen the floor show and Looney Tunes
> and now it's Time for a more-
> practical first lesson in Framing, Point of view,
> Shooting, actual Filming, Editing and sound
> recording – introduction to the Production process.
> You! BUCKET BOY…!

He looks at names on a group photo stuck on the Lecturer's desk

> THOMAS MERRIMAN…(Then whispers)
> CHUBBY CHEEKS, is more-like it. MISTER
> MERRIMAN, after you mop up your mess please go
> and set up the Red Camera. GONERIL…yikes
> (muttered) you can assist him. You other GUYS
> move the rest of the Sound gear and Lights to the
> designated set up station areas marked on the floor
> of the STUDIO next door. I'd like you ladies to
> set up the KEY lighting as per the instructions are
> on the work sheets that JENN gave you and those on
> the side wall, This all takes team work.

MIKE is angry with him and calls him outside for a word while the STUDENTS all head into the Production Room to set up.

SCENE.INT. ACTING ROOM WITH VIEW TO PRODUCTION ROOM.DAY

The two stand talking. In an adjoining room and out of view, WENDY is marking papers and suddenly hears them talk. They don't know she's there

> **MICK**
>
> I hadn't finished my teaching my class yet SLOANE
> Where do you get off calling "TIME" on my lesson?

SLOANE

There wasn't anything remotely resembling teaching or learning going on there that I saw. And then that last inexplicable water show! Fuck me! That looked like you instructing them in Stand-up Comedy techniques for Amateur night. This is a *SLOANE) practical course AS WELL as a theoretical one you TOOL and this University requires bona fide ACADEMICS (SLOANE) to teach the courses, not some.. MICKEY MOUSEschool teacher.

MIKE shifts his stance aggressively and clenches his fists. SLOANE flinches.

MIKE

You and I need to resolve this you DIPSTICK GRUB. And after the FILM Festival in twelve weeks' time we WILL so this. You have the effrontery to criticize me! You call yourself a DIRECTOR, yet you make nothing but violent dross for impression-able adolescents and offer them Nothing of substance. You don't live in a moral world and you peddle the worst kind of audio visual faeces any low life company could crap-out. No wonder you took this job:Yeah, I discovered most of the main Studios gave you an unofficial three year "Leave of Absence Pass" for your moronic booze-induced outburst at the Golden Globes. You couldn't write a screenplay of value if your life depended on it.

SLOANE (SEETHING)

AND YOU'RE A FAILED AND BITTER SECOND- RATE HACK, O'LEARY. I'D BET YOU BLUE POLES TO A BIG BANANA POSTCARD FROM COFFS HARBOUR...IF YOU AND I SUBMITTED ORIGINAL-SCRIPTS TO OUR

UPCOMING SLOANE (CONT)

BUSHRANGER FILM FESTIVAL to the All Comers Open Script Competition, I'd win; or at least place in the top three, and ahead of you. I'd also bet you wouldn't even reach the top three. Remember that all Writers' names will be hidden from THE JUDGES, till the winner is chosen. Your overblown Rep for one average failed feature flick won't count for Diddly Squat.

WENDY listens intently and switches on Record on her mobile

MIKE

You've got yourself a bet, BILGEWATER. I'll bet you five grand I place in the top three, and ahead of you at worst

SLOANE

Uh! Uh! No way you're getting out of it that easy. Let's make it interesting: More like $50K! The 1st prize in the competition is $1 MILLION, after all, and even second is $250K. What's the matter MC FLY? Chicken?

MIKE blanches.

And one more thing: the loser has to apologize to the winner and state publicly he thinks the winner is a truly talented Writer and Director.

SLOANE reaches out to shake hands to cement the bet. But the hand-shake becomes a test of strength which MIKE eventually wins. It makes SLOANE even angrier.

SLOANE

I'm guessing you also don't know half these students paid $1.000.000 a piece to do this course. Only six of them are here on merit.

MIKE looks shocked.

Now I have to go teach something useful to these dopes. Well, my JULIE's the exception of course.

MIKE

And that's another thing: don't belittle any of my students again in my hearing! MERRIMAN's a good kid and whip-smart. And you also need to know the three of us have PERCY SLATER's total support what's more, and we agreed your role was mostly setting up our first Film Festival and teaching the Master Class

He almost chokes on the word MASTER

in Directing. MASTER…HA! You couldn't Direct traffic in a carpark!

His voice wavers as he says the last bit.

So neither DORIAN nor I, or JENN, either, are to have you interrupt our classes anymore without our permission? Get it? AND WHY THE HELL DON'T you

MIKE

understand how hard it is for JULIE having her Dad here in the first place without you acting like a prize scrotum, when people are whispering "Nepotism", is beyond me? Your barging into classes you're not involved with and embarrassing will inevitably lose your daughter to you unless you wise up.

SLOANE

FCUK you're a hypocrite! You don't know shit, and your own kids rarely see you from what JENN said! You and I will definitely have it out before this Christmas O'LEARY: and that's a promise.

MIKE

From what I've seen you're not very good at keeping promises.

MIKE laughs. SLOANE shows him the finger and exits. WENDY glares at her Father and softens as she looks at MIKEINT. SEMINAR ROOM FILM ACADEMY.FOLLOWING WEEK.

MIKE (HOLDING STUDENT SUBMISSIONS)

Well I've read all your Short Film Treatment submissions alright and picked what I think

While excited, they look bewildered by the WORKLOAD are the most promising three – a psychological thriller, and a magic reality story.

One's expensive and you are going to have to animate it with assistance from an ex Disney Animator hired by the Academy. We've also hired a professional Sound expert for all three films to assist you. So without further ado let's hear one of the three finalists, "ASTRAL BOY" by STEVE SANDERS AND MOSHE…ERM SONNY . And another thing, GONERIL you have given me virtually Nothing to date so right now I'd like you to give me a middling idea outline for a short film.. from any genre, before MR SANDERS tells us his.

Nothing fazes her and she makes up a story on the spot.

GONERIL

It's a black comedy. I got the idea for it in SINGAPORE on my one day stop over flying to Melbourne. You see, the CHINESE love to gamble, so the Government had to charge $100 entry fee JUST for them to gain entry to the casino to deter their reckless betting. So, in my story a smart THAI GAL named FUK YU.

MIKE'S SPEECHLESS

AMAL (INTERJECTING)

That's totally racist crap GONERIL!!

GONERIL (UNDETERRED)

It's not! It's Thai-Chinese and I found the name in a Bangkok phone book. It's funny because it's true. Anyhoo, BUM FUK – or just plain FUK, or even FUK YU as her friends call her (EYEBALLING AMAL) opens a truth in Advertising business Called BIG NASTY: THE TRUE GAMBLERS' SURPRISE SHOP.

MIKE and JENN are speechless gobsmacked GOBSM

The entry fee is $30 non-refundable and you enter at your own risk: They scan visitors' Drivers Licences or Passports onto a waiver indemnity document as they enter. Passing through one at a time they get a soft half assed kick in the bum Kick from a shadowy figure in slippers in the first room, a custard pie in the face …

IKE stares at her in wide eyed astonishment.

GONERIL (CONT)

in the second room, hear a recording of an approaching hungry growling animal in the third dark room, step in some phoneydog food and get a hose down as they exit the last room. It's a Goddam Gold mine is what it is and as a short film it would fly! ANYHOO, the GAL makes a MOTZA and there are endless queues. It's just a mysterious and poorly lit shop with four different darkish rooms visitors pass through till reaching a door and pathway back to the main street. VISITORS' are pushed though… at 5 per minute. And those who've gambled and gone through don't warn the others as they're too embarrassed. . And relieved at the same time. Grateful even, for surviving. It's a story about Capitalism, human gullibility and how even how dumb asses can become millionaires.

She looks pleased with herself but it's a bluff

MIKE (LOST FOR WORDS)

At the end of this class you and JENN and I are going to have a very serious talk about what's expected of you in this course GONERIL! Savvy? So..

He looks at his notes

No one seems to be tackling the horror genre and we need someone to make one

SHORT IN .. WOLFGANG & BUI HUONG

That would be Us. We call it "SOMETHING IN THE WATER. It's A shark story about retarded farmer with a sharkphobia who thinks they might be in the bath or maybe swimming pools. In the film a bronze whaler is being transported in salt water pool on the back of a huge truck and he falls out of building into the truck, and……

Everyone makes a cringing face at this story. WOLFGANG picks up script pages from in front of him, shuffles them and starts the narration MERRIMAN sees/projects the whole film on the main screen in the room, complete with wild track and apposite mood music.

SLOANE

I've heard worse. But not since the Berlin Wall came down. And if I hear one more bloody shark story..I swear…Night of the Shark, JAWS 1-6, SHARKNADO, and I fully expect to see SHARKS ON A PLANE, AND MY FAIR SHARK and Shark Man in cinemas soon! AND READ HOW TO PRESENT A SCREENPLAY FOR GOD'S SAKE! Okay, who and what was the runner up?

OK STEVE, and SONNY…start your story please..

JUSTIN

Erm, excusem moi MIKE, but any any chance I could cut it before these guys "take the stage"?

MIKE nods assent as JUSTIN explains

JUSTIN

Thank you..its not in a script form just yet and was a story my Dad told me about this old bloke he met when he was younger and working for a few months up in the high country. He had known an old fisherman up there after meeting him at the pub. The old feller was well liked but was dying at the start of the story and the pub owner's wife told Dad

JUSTIN (CONT)

how she got really emotional while looking after the old bloke for the last hours o his life shared with the old man's two best mates. I thought the only way the story could work would be if I were the narrator after I commissioned a decent animator to illustrate the final moments of his life. Does that sound possibly acceptable?"

JUSTIN looks at MIKE who raises his eyebrows at the class to garner their opinions and they all nod agreement that it is fine and JUSTIN gratefully gives them the thumbs up and begins.

JUSTIN

Come in Number

Had old Robbie been able to look down on the three of them sitting around his bed in the Budawang Hotel waiting for him to die, he would have been amused.

Those sharing the death-watch were Mavis Phillips, licensee, cook, barmaid, and Robbie's two fishing mates, Johnny Pell and Con the Greek. Mavis sat quietly, patiently, but Johnny Pell and Con were uneasy and restless.

Robbie was the hotel's only permanent guest. His room, one of three on the street side of the upstairs corridor, also opened onto the verandah which ran the length of the hotel.

JUSTIN (CONT)

The room was small and sparsely furnished. It contained a wardrobe, bed and a cluttered bedside table. On one wall, brackets supported a fly rod and a spinning rod in the place where a mantelpiece had once provided ornamentation above a now-blocked-off fireplace. On the old hearth, a pair of hip waders lay alongside a canvas satchel with a cotton hat pushed carelessly beneath the flap and an open metal box with shelves full of flies and lures, hooks and lines and, indeed, all the paraphernalia of a long time fisherman.

A curtain covered the door to the verandah and a holland blind did a window. Outside, rain drummed on the galvanised iron roof of the old weatherboard hotel and a gusting wind drove flurries of rain against the window of Robbie's room. Distant thunder grumbled and somewhere a door banged, and banged again.

The curtains also hid the late afternoon view of the deserted main street with its straggle of shops and the ow of gnarled and twisted peppercorn trees which provided the town centre with summer shade. Also hidden by the driving rain were the fields of stubble behind the huddle of house and, further away, the heavily timbered flanks of the main upland range.

Downstairs in the bar, a few regulars enjoyed the warmth from the log fire and the relative peace that would last only until the workers from the timber mill beyond the stockyards ended their days toil. They would pour into the bar rough and loud,

JUSTIN (CONT)

bringing the smell of wet woollens and sweat and the bitter cold of a high-country winter evening, their mouths full of oaths and laughter.

Reg Phillips, the barman and husband of Mavis, moved a desultory cloth slowly over a beer ring on the counter. Above his head, a few hardy flies moved casually to avoid the four blades of the ceiling fan as it cut slow swathes through tendrils of cigarette smoke. He was hoping that Mavis would be back in the bar before the rush.

Mavis sat in a cane chair beside Robbie's bed, holding his thin, brown hand and watching his shadowed face, lit by the meagre efforts of the single bulb suspended above the bed, as the life drained from him.

A woman of late years, she had known Robbie from before the war. He had returned to Budawang with a small pension and had moved into the hotel, supplementing his income with odd jobs around town. He was liked by everyone: a nice old man whose passing would be regretted for a moment and then forgotten.

On the other side of the bed, Johnny Pell and Con sat uncomfortably and unwillingly on chairs brought up from the kitchen. Both were long-time residents of Budawang and long-time intimates of Old Robbie by reason of a shared passion for fishing the beautiful and largely untouched rivers and creeks of the high country behind the town.

JUSTIN (CONT)

Mavis's eyes strayed to the companions with whom she was to share Robbie's death and, not for the first time, wondered at the quirk of circumstances that drew the three of them together: Old Robbie, courtly and civilised, while Johnny and Con were a pair of disreputable, drunken layabouts whose only saving grace was Robbie's acceptance of them. She knew that they were as fond of Robbie as she was and that his death would leave a gap in their lives that they, probably, would never be able to fill. Con glanced up and caught her eye. He shrugged broad shoulders. "Poor old Robbie," he said softly, making a spare gesture with his hands. "D'you think anyone will mind if I take his fishing rods?"

Johnny Pell, stirred by Con's declaration of intent and to avoid being deprived of his share, sat forward on his chair, eyes narrowed and voice belligerent. "Yeah, and I want his waders and his lures."

Mavis looked at them over the still figure in the bed. She knew they were trying to express feelings for which they did not have the words. "He'd want you both to share his things," she said. "You were his best friends."

She looked down at Robbie, wondering if he even knew that they were there. Death was very close.

Robbie had not heard the interchange. He was walking down the grass slope just above the sheep track that skirted the Black Wattle Hill. The air was

JUSTIN (CONT)

crisp and there was the smell of earth left wet by overnight spring showers.

Above him, the new-risen sun was golden through the mist.

The day held promise and he glanced about him as he walked, full of the pleasures of the bush and in anticipation of the river below. It ran darkly, part-hidden by overhanging ti-tree, but soon the water would catch the sun and the river would come alive. He dropped down the hill through wet grass avoiding blackberries and using the proliferation of wattle saplings to slow his descent. He emerged from the shadow of the hill into sunlight and there, ahead, was the first of the pools he planned to fish.

A massive boulder, lichen-covered, narrowed the river at its upstream end and slate-gray water swung clear and fast around it. The ban had been deeply undercut and somewhere in that deep, dark water, sheltered from the current, there would be a trout, its fins barely moving as it watched the big slow swirl of water as the river shelved over gravel towards the sedges on the opposite bank.

Beyond the boulder, Robbie could see the sunlight spreading across the next pool upstream and shafts of light through the ti-tree etched patterns on the grass and water-weed in the shallows. Fish wee rising in the still waters to insects moving from the weed that prospered in an area where the bank had collapsed.

JUSTIN (CONT)

Robbie swuatted in a hollow behind the bank while he studied the pool and prepared his rod. Then he moved slowly and carefully towards a clearing well below the big rock where there was room to cast.

His first effort was a ranging shot and his line fell across the edge of the big rock. He cast again -feeding out the line as the rod flexed under his hand and the tiny brown and red fly soared beyond the rock to land delicately in the swirl of water waiting its turn to run the narrows.

Once, twice, it circled before joining the current to drop over the small pressure wave and into the lower pool. Then it vanished, Robbie waited a long moment before lifting the tip of the rod and striking. He felt the power of the fish as his rod bowed and he retrieved line quickly as the fish paused to consider its situation. Then it ran downstream and the line sliced through the water towards the far bank with just enough drag on the reel to tire the fish. It turned when it reached the bank before fleeing further downstream towards the reeds and the safety of tangled limbs of a fallen willow.

Robbie turned the fish just before it reached the refuge. It was only then that he saw it. The fish threw itself from the water, fighting desperately to throw the hook – gleaming, twisting brown trout – vibrantly alive and full of fight. He played the fish with care, using his line as if it were cotton and – slowly at first – retrieving line and releasing it, he forced the fish towards him.

JUSTIN (CONT)

At the end it was beaten. It came to him in a slow, reluctant sweep, fin above the surface of the water. Robbie saw its real dimensions and was delighted. "I knew we'd meet soon," he said affably.

Just for a moment he thought there was someone peering over his shoulder he glanced quickly around but there was no one.

He unclipped the folded landing net from his belt and flicked it open. His eyes returned to the fish, now exhausted and moving every slowly through the long tendrils of water-weed almost within reach.

He watched it turn its side in the final surrender and, as it did so, the sunlight caught the rich sweep of red, brown and orange speckling that mottled its flanks like jewels and the deep, sombre grey-green of its back.

Robbie new that he was not going to kill the fish. He knelt on the bank, placing his rod and landing net beside him. Pensive, the morning sun warming his back, he looked at the river flowing past. Shafts of sunlight through the trees lit the water and were, themselves, alive with whirling insects. He heard magpies warbling in the eucalyptus branches above him and the 'plop' as a water rat dropped from a log down by the reeds. Before him, the water-grass waving gently around it, lay the great trout. He reached forward to draw the fish nearer so that he could release it from his line. "Ah!" he said. "How beautiful you are."

JUSTIN (CONT)

When Old Robbie withdrew his hand from Mavis's light grasp and reached both arms towards the forty-watt bulb hanging from the fly-spotted ceiling, Johnny Pell gasped and crossed himself and Con the Greek started, as if to rise, so that the legs of his chair squeaked on the linoleum. But Mavis held up her hand and he stilled.

Robbie's face was alight with pleasure. "How beautiful you are," he said. His eyes were open then but he was looking at something beyond the walls of the Budawang Hotel. Smiling, his eyes closed and his life ended.

Mavis stood up stiffly, her eyes wet with tears, and she drew the sheet up over Robbie's face. Johnny ad Con stood too, Johnny knocking over his chair.

"Well," said Mavis softly, not pretending to smile, "we've lost a friend." And because her two companions appeared stunned by events, she sought to ease their shock.

"He wouldn't want you to mourn over him, you know. You'd please him best, the pair of you, by going fishing tomorrow as usual – the rain will have passed and the fresh water will make them active."

Johnny appeared to notice her again. He shook his head and looked down at his hands. "I'm not going fishing. I'm going to church – that's where

JUSTIN (CONT)

I'll be on Sundays from now on. I heard what Robbie said and I saw his face!"

"Me too," said Con the Greek, embarrassed and not meeting Mavis's eyes. "It mightn't be too late for me neither.

SANDERS & MOSHE ALTERNATE

Okay here goes nothing! It's a first draft attempt at a lightweight comedy about ASTRAL TRAVEL. I called it ASTRAL BOY or alternatively, "Have Bun Will Travel". It probably needs to be animated, but I'd prefer to use real actors and green screen if I can get a decent budget for it as I set some of it on an island, where I had holiday a few years back. Just a heads up...you foreign STUDENTS need to know New Zealanders – or KIWIS - pronounce "e" as "i", so that they would say "SIX IN THE CITY" not SEX IN THE CITY.

MERRIMAN's imagination projects it onto the screen featuring most of his classmates in animated form. JULIE is impressed by SANDERS and is clearly now in full competition with STEPHANIE for SANDERS' attention. He seems conflicted about both of them.
RALPH NELSON, (an animated MERRIMAN looking very portly in a fat suit-covered by an old tweed suit, and thick glasses) hurries along a city street carrying a briefcase, glancing at his watch every few seconds. RALPH suddenly stops in exhaustion. He's "hit the wall" – at a travel agency featuring the PACIFIC ISLANDS in the display window, an advertisement for POLYNESIAN PARADISE AIRWAYS. He's transfixed by a poster photograph of a beautiful POLYNESIAN WOMAN (played by an animated (BUI

HUONG) sitting in a wicker chair on an idyllic beach, the blue Pacific lapping at her feet. She's tantalizing and RALPH's daydream stops suddenly when a very large Polynesian Travel Agent emerges from the office. Mild mannered RALPH'S in a lather and accosts the man.

> **RALPH**
>
> Erm, excuse me Sir - would you by any chance know where that Island is and how I can get there?

The man's a fat animated Polynesian SONNY. He laughs at the picture a

> **APELESA (NEW ZEALAND ACCENT)**
>
> Mate, it might as well be NEVERLAND even though POLYNESIAN PARADISE AIRWAYS do call it AI'OFORI Island! It's a fable to you though, because they don't want people to know where it is. That would totally destroy its mystique. So, unless you've got your own set of wings... ! She's some beautiful girl though, eh BRO? She's part of the advertising fable too.

RALPH is an emotional mess so the ISLANDER indulges him

> Look, all I can tell you is that it's a remote little Atoll somewhere between the COOK ISLANDS and TONGA . But you're never going to get there cos it's
> off the main sea route - it'd be like finding a microscopic green spec in a hundreds and

                    APELESA (CONT)

   thousands packet. My advice: Get yourself an
   AUSTRALIAN GIRLFRIEND ...and hey, it's not my
   APELESA business, but if you lost some weight,
   pumped some iron and got rid of the four eyes
   bifocals! You never know..

He heads off up the Street and RALPH winces at his portly image in the window before hurrying away. EXT. CITY STREET DAY RALPH looks very unfit as he shuffles up the street and he is short of breath when he stops again for a few seconds to read the signs in the windows of a shop front he passes. The first reads: STOP MAKING A SPECTACLE OF YOURSELF! SEE US AT TRULY EYEFUL LASER SURGERY AND ALWAYS LOOK YOUR BEST.

INT.EXT.GYMNASIUM.DAY
At the adjoining building he stops at a shop front and peers at the sign BODY TEMPLE GYMNASIUM Make Your Muscles Bulge and Change Your Life Forever. Underneath in bold lettering another smaller sign reads NO LARD ASSES! RALPH makes another face and seems to take a non-verbal inventory. He glances at his watch and on a whim, mounts the stairs. CUT TO

SCENE.INT.GYM.DAY
RALPH signs a gym membership form with a well-buffed "Babe" looking on patronizingly.(PLAYED BY AN ANIMATED VERSION OF STEPHANIE)

                    MS BEAUDACIOUS

   Do yous know how ter use gym equipment
   MISTER?

She is too thick to hide her narcissism and when he glances up from the page he is filling in he catches her making a face at a pumped up pneumatic moron: RALPH is a joke to her. As he glances along the wall mirror he realizes the place is full of narcissists. He takes a quick walk around the gym and is delighted to see the picture of the young POLYNESIAN woman on a wall there too, but near the picture is a wall clock that reads 9.00 A.M. He's really late for work and rushes out down the steps and up the street, looking as though he could have a heart attack.

SCENE.EXT.RALPH'S BOOKSHOP.DAY
When he arrives at what is obviously his own book shop - "RARE BOOKS and PRE LOVED BOOKS", his two employees are waiting for him to open up. CHARLENE(ANIMATED VERSION OF STEPHANIE), shy, cute and not GOTHIC in the Animation friendly; and HONG, a punk Chinese Australian part time Uni student female - played in the Animation by BUI HUONG) dressed as a Star Trek character, are waiting patiently for RALPH's arrival and the visual inference is that he is probably never late. There are also a few customers milling round and muttering in annoyance at the tardy opening as he unlocks the security doors

SCENE.INT.BOOK SHOP.DAY
Several DISSOLVES inside the SHOP visually relate a typical day for the staff. The visual construct shows a beautiful little shop that is clearly RALPH's pride and joy.
DISSOLVES of an antique grandfather clock face show the passage of the day. The clock reads 10.00 AM ,11.00 A.M., 11.30 and so on. It's knelling of the hours and loud ticking seem to comprise the main sounds in the shop apart from hushed conversations.

PIXILLATION of HONG, RALPH and CHARLENE go about their day. They are, respectively, sorting books into categories, doing audits, helping customers find what they are looking for and making sales and exchanges at the computer cash register. CLOSE: The grandfather clock reads 12.00 PM

CHARLENE's face is transparent and shows she is in love with RALPH but he barely notices her existence.
ALTERNATING DISSOLVES and PIXILLATION of the day suggests that little ever changes in the daily lives of these three co-workers. PAN TO

SCENE.INT.BOOK SHOP.APPROACHING SUNDOWN.
CLOSE ON the grandfather clock knells 5.00 P.M, and closing time. HONG begins closing the window shutters and CHARLENE LOGS off the computer and packs up her things.

SCENE.INT.BOOK SHOP.DAY

RALPH's annoyed when he hears the shop bell ring. An antique looking woman in period style dress resembles BEATRIX POTTER, when she enters the book-shop holding four books she wishes to sell. CHARLENE and HONG look questioningly at RALPH but he shrugs and nods for them to let her in. HONG locks the door after her as she enters.

INT.BOOK SHOP.DAY

The elderly woman bee lines for RALPH.

MAGGIE

Hello there SNOWBALL. I've brought you some interesting books. Your sign says you buy as well as sell. I'm not too late am I….?

He glances at her curiously for a moment and shakes his head, takes the books and adjusts his glasses. The books show the titles "A Critique of Pure Reason" by the Philosopher EMMANUEL KANT; "PATHS to ENLIGHTENMENT" by various authors; and a first edition of "THE MAGIC PUDDING" by Norman Lindsay. He gives her back the KANT book with a shudder. He opens classic

LINDSAY and sees it's a signed First Edition with letters of the Editor. His honesty and his greed begin to fight.

RALPH

> I'll give you $15 dollars for this KANTbook…it's in fair nick. Not sure about Enlightenment but!

She squints and interrupts him, picking up a PRITTIKIN DIET BOOK book from a display table and holding it up next to the book on Enlightenment.

MAGGIE (HOLDS UP THE DIET BOOK)

> Enlightenment is as important as breathing and loving.So, while PRITIKIN'S' book's about physical Enlightenment it's not much damn use unless you've mastered Emotional Enlightenment first.

She proffers the other book and he gives her a funny look. She has a wry smile as he turns his face to a nearby full length mirror and sees he is unhappy with the body profile he sees. At that moment too, a great shaft of sunlight miraculously shines through a stained glass window onto CHARLENE, enshrining her with a beatific look, and like an epiphany, RALPH sees her as if for the first time and realizes she has a uniquely beautiful face.

RALPH

He's thinking MAGGIE may be deranged

> Okay -yy then, um …. in truth I must admit to some interest in this first copy of "The MAGIC PUDDING" though. How much do you want for it?

CHARLENE's within hearing distance pretending to sort books. She visibly knows it's very valuable and is concerned with RALPH's reaction

MAGGIE

You have a trustworthy face RALPHY

She reads his name tag and takes liberties with it

Whatever you think is a fair price is fine by me.

He catches her eavesdropping and looks closely at MAGGIE and then the book. His honesty gets the better of him. At the register he writes a cheque and she's delighted. Then she seems to look into his soul.

MAGGIE

Oh my sainted aunt! 3000 dollars! I had no idea! You know, it might just be in your interest to check out a unique little booklet in the envelope stuck to page 79 ..Many a time in my life I found it quite an adventurous little read. Consider it a gift.

He's bemused AND TELLS HONG TOLOCKS UP AGAIN AFTER LEAVING.. He turns again at the sound of the shop's bell but MAGGIE's gone. The girls are about to exit when he calls out to them holding the open envelope from Page 79. Inside there's a strange booklet with a title that reads: "Fly By Night: A Beginner's Guide To Astral Travel".

RALPH

Hey you two. Get a load of this pamphlet the old lady left. It's a doozy... and weren't you talking about visiting your parents in Hong Kong before Christmas HONG? This might save you the airfares.

The other two have a chuckle at the title of the pamphlet.

BUIHONG

Taking it from her hands

> Yeah, I'll read it. It'll give me a laughing break from my Uni Physics books.

He departs the shop reading it. DISSOLVE TO

EXT.SHOP.EVENING
RALPH walks along the street with CHARLENE. There is a distance between them but also an awkwardness suggesting he has begun to be attracted to her.
From HER P.O.V RALPH/MERRIMAN fights an urge to gorge as they pass MC DONALD'S but by sheer will power, he moves on and enters a Health Food Shop a few doors up instead.
CHARLENE looks confused and surprised by what is clearly his out-of-character behaviour, and is stunned when they reach the BODY TEMPLE Gymnasium further up the street and he waves good night to her before heading up the stairs to the gym. She's surprised and when she sees her own somewhat portly reflection in the GYM window, she looks at the Gym's opening times and makes an obviously conscious decision to follow his example and then resignedly moves on.

SCENE.INT.HONG'S FLAT. NIGHT.
HONG's eating Chinese food in her little flat and reading the "Astral Travel book. She's also drinking wine and looks to be under the weather. She's mellow enough to be having a go at following the book's instructions as closely as she can even though she is laughing aloud while he does it. She's soon lying prostrate and mouthing an incantation while simultaneously focusing on a large map of SHANGHAI and a sizeable mounted photo of her and her family, the YANGSE River in the background.. DISSOLVE TO
Later she's almost asleep when he reads the last line in the book

HONG
This incantation cannot fully work if attempted under the influence of alcohol or drugs".

She cusses as the map and the photo begin to go out of focus and the room spins. DISSOLVE TO.

INT.EXT.APARTMENT, SKY AND CITY.NIGHT
As the room comes into focus again an unconscious HONG begins to levitate and passes through the window of the second story apartment and out into the night sky. Shortly her body is floating over the Sydney Harbour at a considerable speed. DISSOLVE TO HONG's unconscious body is soon floating down into a busy CHINESE street with restaurants and Chinese delicatessens and the rest, although no one seems to see her. She wakes up momentarily and looks around stunned.

SCENE.EXT.CHINATOWN.NIGHT
She gingerly gets to her feet and stares in amazement at "CHINA" all around her. But when she turns the corner she sees she is only in Chinatown in Sydney, and shakes her head crossly as she pulls out the little booklet from her pocket and reads the line "Will not work if attempted under the influence alcohol". CUT TO

SCENE.INT.EXT.BUS AND CITY STREETS.NIGHT
HONG is looking out a bus window. A little later she gets out at a stop near some apartments...

SCENE.INT. BODY & SOUL GYM.DAY
On the same night in the gym RALPH is running on a treadmill, his eyes fixed on the Polynesian woman in the Airline poster as he runs. APELESA and another powerful looking TONGAN MAN are lifting heavy weights close, they catch him staring at the girl in the picture and grin at each other

APELESA
Good-natured, humorous, but gentle

> You're not still fixated with that girl Bro? I'm sorry, but you? And THAT
> GIRL on THAT island? As likely as me winning a Nobel Prize for PHYSICS.

His friend HORUA is an aggressive type and he lowers his massive weight with apparent ease and strolls over towards RALPH

HORUA

> You got that right APELESA. Mate, you look like you only want THAT GIRL for lunch, or a snack, and even then it'd be after you'd eaten any restaurant's entire main course menu.

RALPH is momentarily wounded but ups the rate on the stationary bike and pedals as if his life depends on it.

RALPH (AS IF HE'S GOT A DEATH WISH)

> I bet I'd have more of a shot than you would BUDDY. Your face closely resembles a KOALA'S CLACKER:

HORUA moves threateningly towards him looking bent on demolishing him but APELESA steps in and drags him away.

HORUA

> Speak to me like that again four eyes and I'll actually insert a Koala in your clacker.

INT.GYMNASIUM.DAY
Early the following morning CHARLENE buys a pear and a yoghurt bar in the Health food shop and approaches the entrance to

the same Gymnasium. From her POV her watch reads 7 A.M and the bimbo is just opening up as she arrives. The woman gives her a look of disapproval but CHARLENE'S face suggests she's decided to give herself a serious make-over.

EXT/INT.BOOK SHOP.DAY
RALPH and CHARLENE are working in the shop when Hong arrives late and holds the Astral book up in the air and waves it around wildly as she explains what happened to her, RALPH excitedly demands the book back.

INT/EXT BOOKSHOP/GYMNASIUM,DAY/NIGHT
A MONTAGE OF SCENES SHOWING TIME PASSING
A series of alternating action scenes and dissolves of Gym visits of CHARLENE and RALPH of which he is blissfully unaware. ethereal SUPER IMPOSED DISSOLVES on the gym wall calendar show them working maniacally in the gym and eating less and less. Warren's gaze is still firmly fixed on the Polynesian beauty on the wall as he trains, but more and more he begins to notice CHARLENE in their workplace.
The calendar displays the fact that it is three months later and CHARLENE and RALPH (MERRIMAN AND STEPHANIE correspondingly) He no longer wears glasses after his laser surgery.

INT.BOOKSHOP.DAY
Inside the book shop he watches her from a distance but is also still fixated on the POLYNESIAN GIRL as he starts to remove a photograph sized reduction of the poster. CHARLENE accidentally comes upon him looking at the picture and looks mortally wounded. He is momentarily dumbfounded at being caught out.

CHARLENE

Who's that girl RALPH? I thought you and I were...!
I thought...

They look at each other mortified. She spies the book headlining "ASTRAL TRAVEL" and understands what he is planning. She departs immediately. He watches her go with a tortured look but when he looks back at the photograph he appears resigned to his Polynesian fantasy.

INT.RALPH'S HOUSE. SUNDAY MORNING .
RALPH has finally resolved to try the journey A'OFORI . He looks philosophical and a little concerned as he studies the book and reads the mantra. Before him is a moderate Polynesian Feast he has concocted consisting of coconut, paw-paw, yams, jack fruit and the like.
He devours most of the food, reads the book in gibberish language andlies down Yoga-like fashion. As his mantra finishes he hears banging at the door. It's CHARLENE.But he can barely keep his eyes open.

CHARLENE

Don't leave. That GIRL'S just a pipe dream. I'm here in the flesh. I'm your reality and I'm available. Please stay.He tries to fight it but drifts off into a deep sleep. She leaves in despair.

Shortly afterwards RALPH's Astral body rises two meters above his bed. A wind comes up and his Astral body floats through the window. It moves drifts at speed like a low flying buzz bomb over Bush, over Seas and islands in an ethereal flight.

EXT. OVER LAND AND SEA TO PACIFIC ATOLL. DAY.
RALPH floats dreamily down onto the idyllic beach in the picture. Slowly he regains consciousness and stands in a dazed fashion.

SCENE.EXT.PACIFIC ATOLL.DAY
In the distance further along the beach he spies the beautiful young Polynesian woman and starts to jog and then run up the beach

towards her as she frolics in the shallows splashing water on her naked breasts. He runs towards her now in slow motion and stands at the water's edge staring at her. Suddenly he hears a strongly KIWI accented voice behind him and turns to find an Advertising crew filming her in the semi buff.

AD DIRECTOR LEE (N.Z ECCENT)

What the fick do Yi think yi're doin' here on our SIT (SET) you bleddy Pervert. Get off our fickin' island BUTTERBALL.

TAMAHINE LARO

In an over-the –top New Zillund accent

Yeah, you fickin' hippopotamic PAKEHA PANSY. Get yer six life somewhere ilse (CONT) and get the fick off our island' less you wanna find your fat arse in OPIN WATER with reef sharks like thet Yenk skin diving couple in thet MovieOPIN WATER!

SCENE.EXT.PACIFIC ATOLL.DAY
RALPH looks as if every skerrick of blood and air has been instantly sucked from his body. He trudges back up the beach near where he landed, removes the ASTRAL book and the remnants of his feast from his back pocket as he goes. He now sits in the sand and begins eating and reciting the mantra. He lies down and drifts off into an unhappy sleep. This time the sun is setting as his body rises and heads over the Pacific back to Australia.

INT/EXT.RALPH'S APARTMENT.DAY
On this occasion the time zone saves him and he awakes just as CHARLENE is still banging on his door trying to stop him leaving. The door opens and they stand looking at each other, both cool and knowing who they really are for the first time since they've known each other

RALPH

To PARAPHRASE what THEY said about
Poor Old KING CHARLES the First, 400 years ago:
I'm the biggest fool in CHRISTENDOM…

CHARLENE

Make that the biggest Tool in ESSENDON and
you're getting close.

RALPH

I'm not going anywhere ever again unless IT'S with
you.

CHARLENE

It was my intention to put fire ants in
Y fronts but I've had a change of heart,
cos I thought you'd never ask and
forgiveness is next to Godliness, right?.

They smile at each other and hug lovingly.

THE END

INT.ACADEMY SEMINAR ROOM DAY.
The class look basically onside with SANDERS' film treatment, as if they can do something decent with the story

MIKE

Well, I suggest you start planning and creating a funding plan. Too many of you here thinking Animation, but I want live action for this one. could do it for a $40K budget. You do have access to green screen and some SFX here at the UNI, and you'll need to film on weekends as it needs to be made and edited within six weeks. I've also organized an excursion for us to an Old West Town that was built for an old TV Western series remake called BACK TO BONANZA. We'll go there to shoot practice scenes for a real Australian Western well make in the New Year.! As a team you'll write it a conventional Western scenes, act in them, and film them within two days followed by a free day in DAYLESFORD town. It's a 2 or 3 hour bus trip from Melbourne . I booked us a hotel there.This isn't a holiday though you'll need to edit it by the following Tuesday. Everyone okay with that?

They're excited by this prospect. MERRIMAN immediately Projects and "sees" his fellow students dressed as western characters: GONERIL the bordello madam; JUSTIN, WOLFGANG and WALLY as gunslinger; SONNY and AMAL as piano and songstress; and BUI HUONG as CALAMITY JANE and so forth.

MIKE

So the other script is "EUCALYPTO" by WALLY and WALLY Only ready ..ish..just ideas at the moment

SLOANE, MIKE and DORIAN and the STUDENTS give WALLY

their attention as he starts his story. MERRIMAN projects this story onto the screen as WALLY tells it.
EUCALYPTO

WALLY

Okay, then…I this is a kids' story but I suppose it's my kind of revisionist History of part of NSW. EUCALYPTO is a magical little town AND a Democratic Republic located in a hidden Somewhere in the hinterland of mid coastal NSW. It was the traditional land of the wisest, most educated and most isolated tribe in Australia. This an adventure and a magic realism TV Pilot and series about childhood, life and the future.

MERRIMAN'S IMAGINATION VISUALLY TRANSLATES HIS WORDS INTO COMPELLING IMAGES

VISION: RUM CORPS Soldiers and clearly high ranking OFFICERS and a PEER of the REALM (LORD MONTAGUE) sit around a campfire in discussion with impressive looking ABORIGINAL WARRIORS and their Leader JABANUNGA WADIMAN. MONTAGUE is obviously despised by the SOLDIERS.
In the background are substantial Aboriginal dwellings and idyllic bush.
WADIMAN'S beautiful and savvy 15 year old daughter MELLA watches the talks in apparent fascination and Catches the eye of Libidinous LORD MONTAGUE.
DISSOLVE TO:

TRACKING: LORD MONTAGUE allegedly going for a "PERAMBULATION" – is actually stalking MELLA. He approaches her in a bushy setting and makes advances. He starts taking off his clothes, little realizing it's a set up. The

REDCOATS, WADIMAN and some WARRIORS catch him in the Act of sexual assault and WADIMAN tells him its DEATH by WADI (CLUB) or total Capitulation.

MONTAGUE agrees to sign documentation bequeathing these lands to the tribe in perpetuity. This is witnessed by the RUM CORPS (in collusion with the GOODABUDGEE tribe)

WALLY

So this all happens in 1809 and as the clever old WADIMAN's expert in English he procures a Crown Letterhead Royal Seal document Endorsing the tribe's traditional rights forever and he's immediately provided the appropriate documentation and a duplicate which were duly signed with two high ranking British officers and a ticket of leave ex LONDON LAWYER /Convict named FINEIGHLER, witnessing it.Over the next two centuries it became home to 400 cheerful souls and A EUTOPIA and SANCTUARY for troubled and lost children where they can live in happiness growing towards a brilliant future in a safe place free from dumb opinionated adults, bullies (any BULLIES who get in there end up on the local BUNYIP's Menu, unless they are truly repentant and changed) :EUCALYPTO kids must leave at 16 and can rarely return. Any bad people managing to get in are "disappeared" by Divine justice: "Biblical" storms; falling trees; giant hail stones; killer bees; turtles dropped by passing eagles landing their heads; by the ravenous Bunyip; or as a result of some accidental mega fauna trampling them or some-such…

Suddenly a fire alarm is set off and the ringing reverberates throughout the building. The class pack up.

MIKE

So far so good mister HARROWER: TO BE CONTINUED!

SC. INT. PRIVATE HIGH ROLLERS ROOM CROWN CASINO. NIGHT

From the POV of a dowdily dressed woman, PERCY SLATER is seen dressed to the nines and seated at a high END poker table. It's clear the stakes are big. He looks confident with his hand and is enjoying a pert breasted gorgeous MODEL massaging the back of his neck.
CLOSE. The watcher is his wife AGNES KELLY SLATER. Surprisingly she seems reflective rather than furious or jealous as she studies the woman touching him so familiarly. She even makes several notes and takes a secretive photo of the woman from another angle with her Mobile before leaving the room.
From another angle VIET MINDER MINH watches these goings-on curiously and when PERCY retires from the table MINH follows him

INT.CROWN CASINO MELBOURNE.NIGHT

MINH follows PERCY SLATER into the rough and tumble sports bar and as there is a big football match on there are quite a few drunks, some cheerful and some aggressive. It's a big crowd and the bouncers look rather frazzled.
CLOSE: A large BOOFHEAD dressed narcissistically to display his gym-sculpted muscles bumps into PERCY, spilling his drink.

PERCY

Hey careful MATE, this is a new suit..

The BOOFHEAD is spoiling for a fight and takes a swing at

PERCY, but MINH is impossibly fast and grabs the bully's wrist, twisting it and bearing down forcing him to his knees. He whispers in the man's ear.

MINH

Name is MINH. MINH happy to tie reef knot in your right arm if you not say very sorry to gentleman when MINH let you stand-up. Drunk man understand MINH's English talk?

MINH applies momentary pressure and the man's face shows he's in excruciating pain as he nods enthusiastically. When he stands up two of the bouncers glance at them but it happened so fast they missed it.

DRUNKEN BULLY (VERY CONTRITE)

Um, I'm sorry for my haymaker sir. I think I had too much to drink.

He looks fearfully at MINH to see if his apology was adequate. MINH nods and waves him away. PERCY is very grateful and offers his hand.

PERCY

Well thank you very much for your most welcome assistance mate. My name's PERCY: PERCY SLATER.

MINH

My name MINH. From MY DINH MOT HANOI. In VIETNAM. MINH pleased he can help you.

PERCY

Let me buy you a drink. I could definitely use a BLOKE like you on my staff.

PERCY leads him over to the bar and orders beers.

PERCY

So, MINH, a handy MINDER like you... I don't know your salary in NAM but how does $1500 a week sound for starters? And, out of interest, have you ever tried any Cage Fighter.

SCENE. INT. OLD CHARTER BUS COUNTRY HIGHWAY. MORNIN

From WALLY HARROWER's POV the bus travels through picturesque bush hills and farmland. SLOANE lies on the back seat wearing headphones and listening to music. All the students except WOLFGANG and STEPHANIE (APPARENTLY NOW BOINK BUDDIES) as well as MIKE and JENN are watching a series of classic western DVDs on the mounted flat screen TV.

INT.EXT.COUNTRY TOWN AND 1880 WESTERN THEME TOWN.

At dusk the bus pulls into a decent looking hotel motel in a beautiful little country tourist town. While all inside look worn out, they are visibly cheered by the high-standard of the place. SLOANE disembarks and heads for Reception and JENN and MIKE address them.

MIKE

Okay there's two or three per suite: Females in separate rooms from males. All we ask of you is that you all behave responsibly. No rock-star antics with furnishings, no drugs...and go easy on the bar fridge and room service. Remember that your name goes with you into the future so if you want a good rep in this gossip-ridden industry, earn it by doing right. There is a nice pub thatserves good food a block-away and a few of us are going there if you want to join us. Otherwise...Good night.

GONERIL

Stay loose Poppa Goose. We won't charge any Wagyu beef or Chateau Neuf Du Pape to your room...
  He makes a dubious face.

JENN

It's an early start tomorrow so you'll all get a reminder phone call at 6am. Finish showers and breakfast by 6.45 And we drive the two miles to into history and a reconstruction of 1880 "Dodge" city or Tombstone or somewhere. Re read the acting notes before bed please..

JUSTIN

What notes would that be JENN?

JENN shakes her head in exasperation.

MIKE (FEIGNING ANGER)

Grrr!

WOLFIE

Do you think you could tuck me in tonight JENN

She flicks his ear and grins.
  JENN
  Sure – Into an airless WOODEN coffin if that works for you.

MIKE gives him a "watch your manners" look. They all head off with the filming gear and bags and JENN goes to Reception to collect their keys.

INT.COUNTRY PUB NEAR WESTERN TOWN.NIGHT.

An hour later some of the group has spread out into a couple of adjoining booths. WENDY'S talking to MIKE . They're also watching the STUDENTS somewhat suspiciously.

WENDY

I get the impression you and my mother might have been more than class mates when you were at University? Or is that my vivid imagination.

MIKE grins and looks at JENN across from them and just out of hearing.

MIKE

Mea culpa. But pretty much all the guys were in love with JENN back then. Your DAD got lucky.

WENDY is wide-eyed and glances at her mum

WENDY

Really?

JENN (CALLING OUT TO THEM)

What are you telling her Mr O'LEARY. Don't believe half of what that reprobate tells you WENDY.

WENDY (QUIETLY TO MICK)

I thought my father was the reprobate!

MIKE scans the students around them and smiles approvingly at JUSTIN and BERNADETTE sitting nearby and getting on brilliantly.

MIKE

Wow that's a pairing I'd never have imagined

WENDY

I did! She's old fashioned and a sweet homebody at heart. And he's just discovering what a breath of fresh air she is after the phonies he usually dates.

MIKE's glances at them realizes she's right.

INT/EXT.1880 BONANZA WESTERN TOWN. DAYLESFORD. DAY

The bus in the background as the town's manager greets them with his 7 year old young son and his dog.

HARRY

G'day, you fellas must be MIKE and BRYCE...and JENN. I'm HARRY. This lad is my son ALLAN and his dog SHANE.

They all shake hands.

MIKE (SMILING AT THEM)

Hi guys..and these are our motley crew.

They follow father and son on a quick orientation of the town and surrounds.

HARRY

So that's the saloon over there, next door's the bordello currently in long term hibernation.... Down the street there's a barn and the BLACKSMITH. Next door is what we call the O.K Corral and well-behaved saddle horse for each of you. They're all placid except DIABALO the PALOMINO.. WHO'S NO PAL A MINE O Stay right away from him..um there's a barber shop and general store over

HARRY (CONT)
there and a hotel and cafe behind me.. And over here we've got change rooms and lockers and all your costumes and such-like for the day.

He leads them into adjoining rooms male and female where they find a vast array of period western costumes, mock hand guns and rifles and holsters they each choose from.

EXT.WESTERN TOWN.DAY
They emerge in ones and twos onto Main Street looking like the cast from TRUE GRIT or WYATT EARP. BERNADETTE and JUSTIN are dressed as a pioneering couple and carry hand held digital cameras and mount trail bikes provided by HARRY.. MERRIMAN has a hand held HD digital hand held camera and watches as MIKE and SLOANE glare at each other looking like a couple of gunslingers. He plays Spaghetti western music into his headphones. JULIE and BUI HUONG are dressed like mid-19th century hookers, WALLY is dressed as an UNDERTAKER and WOLFGANG as a blacksmith. MERRIMAN as a preacher, STEPHANIE as a temperance league woman, AMAL and SONNY (MOSHE) are gunslingers and STEPH makes a very fetching Indian SQUAW.
HARRY and Jimmy join them and walk them to the corral.

EXT.CORRALL. WESTERN.TOWN.DAY
The others mount their horses and either trot around uncomfortably or canter according to their confidence and experience.

MIKE (DRESSED LIKE C.EASTWOOD IN HANG EM HIGH)
Okay, you have your notes and your designated technical or acting role..except for THOMAS.

MERRIMAN has his leg in plaster

MIKE (CONT)

It's 8 A.M now and the bus will take us back to the hotel at about 6 PM. After that it's free time till 0800 tomorrow when we'll be homeward bound. Your brief was to act and shoot scenes inspired by the storylines I gave you of The Sheepman, Red River, Soldier Blue, She Wore a Yellow Ribbon, SHANE, The SEARCHERS and any other famous westerns.. Especially JOHN FORD ones. Okay then…away you go.. except for THOMAS. You and I MR MERRIMAN can hole up in the Saloon and you can work on a screenplay. Break a leg now everybody… well not you THOMAS.

All But MERRIMAN ride off in groups, as lingers leaning on his crutches

MERRIMAN

What will you and BRYCE shoot MIKE?

He grins enigmatically and SLOANE answers for him

SLOANE (DRESSED IN OLD TIME HIGH WHITE HAT AND CLOTHES FROM 1950)

We'll be doing a IMPROV scene from SUGARFOOT Meets the TERMINATOR. I'm playing the Terminator…so THOMAS, why don't you just mosey off to yonder Dry Gulch Saloon like Dennis Weaver's (CONT) limping Deputy in that old TV show "GUNSMOKE"

MERRIMAN

But you haven't got a camera or a CAMERAMAN.. ohrr..

He realizes they're going to have it out violently.

MERRIMAN (CONT)

Well, can I at least fix you both an early morning snifter..erm, libation or heart starter. I trained as a BARMAN as an Undergraduate student in Cambridge.

The men look at each other for a second.

SLOANE

Why not!

MIKE

Sure, one'll get me started and It'll help anaesthetize you after I've rearranged your facial structure, HOLLYWOOD. Give you JOHN MERRICK ELEPHANT MAN makeover. It'll be an improvement!

MIKE gives him a photo of poor JOHN MERRICK. They casually follow the slow moving MERRIMAN to the bar.

SCENE.INT.SALOON.DAY
Inside the bar is a replica or the picaresque saloons of so many western films. Harry's in there tidying up and gives MERRIMAN the nod to pour the MEN a drink, so he pours two big beers and turns his back on them to fix a snack, but when he glances at them in the mirror fortuitously catches SLOANE dropping a tablet in MIKE'S drink SLOANE drains his drink as a challenge for MIKE to match him, which he does.

MERRIMAN

Another, gentlemen?

They glance at each other again. It's a test.

> SLOANE

One more won't affect my right hook.

> MICK

Your right hook couldn't knock the froth off a beer.

MERRIMAN queries if they want seconds and MIKE nods "yes" to another beer,. MERRIMAN surreptitiously removes TWO TYLENOL from his pocket and breaks them over both beers and then ferries them over to the table. This time they drink a little more slowly. DISSOLVE TO:It quickly generates into a drinking competition before the fight.

> SLOANE

And I can drink you under the table to boot!

> MICK

You and two dehydrated CAMELS!

INT.SALOON.DAY
JENN arrives hot and thirsty with her work satchel and in a moment notes the nine empty schooner glasses in front of each of the rivals. She exchanges querying looks with a smiling MERRIMAN and understands the score.
CLOSE on a wall clock shows 10 minutes to midday.

> MICK (SLURRING SOMEWHAT NOW)

Ok HOLLYWOOD, time's up. It's noon. HIGH NOON!

HARRY suddenly arrives carrying two loaded-paint-ball guns, which Sloane appears happy with as he looks as if he's having second thoughts about fisticuffs.
As MIKE follows SLOANE out through the swinging saloon doors MERRIMAN puts money in the juke box and as he looks out at the

main street through the saloon doors he sees the two LECTURERS face each other belligerently as the first line of FRANKIE LANE's song HIGH NOON echoes through the room JENN laughs out loud and head for the bar, behind which HARRY now stands.

JENN

Well I might as well join them seeing it's kiddies' play day. Can I have a SARSPARILLA on the rocks please BARMAN.

SCENE.EXT. MAIN STREET.DAY
From MERRIMAN'S POV the two combatants are definitely somewhat "out of it", the alcohol and medication slowing them down considerably. MERRIMAN sees their actions in slow motion and as he looks up and down the street he starts to see it all as a melange of famous scenes from Western shoot outs.
At one end of the street a horseman (as in the preacher character in PALE RIDER) virtually manifests like a spirit, bracketed between to taller buildings. When MERRIMAN looks again it is the little boy ALAN "sitting astride" a hobby horse with his trusty dog SHANE. The boy trots between the buildings and disappears.

EXT. MAIN STREET WESTERN TOWN.DAY
For a moment MERRIMAN has an imagination overload and down the street in speeding succession ride two INDIANS doing stunt riding, jumping over the horse as it gallops, standing on it and so on. Next come a series of galloping cowboys dressed as early era cowboys, TOM MIX, HOPALONG CASSIDY, The LONE RANGER etc. Suddenly MERRIMAN "glimpses" scenes of the old movie full on gunfight at the OK Corral at the end of the street the street.
The ADVERSARIES are now 10 meters apart when SLOANE shoots his paint gun and it hits MIKE in the stomach, enraging him. MIKE runs at SLOANE but he's so wasted it seems to take forever for him to reach his nemesis. Jump cuts go from face to

face showing MIKE's steely eyes and SLOANE's fear. When the shot becomes a wide shot again it's in comic slow motion as MIKE reaches SLOANE, ducks under his wild haymaker and grabs him by the throat as they simultaneously collapse to the ground as the tranquilizers and alcohol take over. SLOANE is instantly asleep and just before he falls asleep too, MIKE opens one ground level eye and spies JENN AND MERRIMAN watching him above the top of the saloon doors. JENN shakes her head at him with a wry grin as if he's a boy who'll never grow up.

SCENE.INT/EXT.BUS IN WESTERN TOWN.
As the bus slowly drives out of town MIKE and SLOANE are at opposite ends of the vehicle, half asleep. MICK's window is open and he watches and listens as the young boy ALAN's dog SHANE runs away from him towards the bus. The little boy calls out to him as he runs:

ALLAN

Don't go SHANE. I love you SHANE.

SLOANE is late and jogs towards the idling bus, but SHANE takes a disliking to him and attacks his lower-leg and won't let go of his trousers. SLOANE curses and swears but can't shake him. The STUDENTS on the bus think it's hilarious and as the bus slowly drives off, SLOANE jumps on the bottom step and kicks the dog away. MIKE sees JULIE'S embarrassment, and shuts up the STUDENTS with a with a stern look.

SCENE.INT. SYDNEY CASINO. FIGHT CLUB ROOM.DAY
The diminutive but lethally tough MINH is in the fight cage up against a man mountain. There is only a small audience of high rollers and they're all betting big bucks on the giant. PERCY bets big on Minh and then sits in the front seat and gives MINH the thumbs up. It's clear PERCY'S now his MANAGER.
The fight is amazing as MINH is impossibly fast and climbs the

cage as quickly as a monkey "on speed ". He runs rings around the giant and then disables him and wins within two minutes. PERCY couldn't be happier and wins a small fortune.

INT. STATE ART GALLERY.DAY.
JULIE and BUI HUONG are late to DORIAN's peripatetic lesson at the Art Gallery of Victoria foyer. JULIE sees DORIAN pacing impatiently and theatrically in front of the other ten STUDENTS sitting on the raised stone border of a small inside fountain. They look dispirited. DORIAN looks explosive as he sees them coming towards him.

DORIAN

So generous of you to grace us with
your presence MS SLOANE..Ms BUI HUONG.. I know that in your elite New York College it might have been fashionable for young female FASHIONISTAS to be late for their classes Ms SLOANE, but in this country and in a course of this prestige level, it is essential that you be on time. Every (DORIAN) time. It is a serious discourtesy to your LECTURER and your PEERS and if it happens again there will be consequences.Are we clear?

JULIE

Crystal!

She intentionally uses the AMERICAN cliche and elicits a nasty look from him.

DORIAN

Let's get this show on the road then

The group stand in front of a quality landscape painting. STUDENTS gather round him holding note pads and pens, most wearing small backpacks. JULIE has a white stick and dark glasses feigning blindness.

DORIAN

Mr SANDERS...please enlighten us in succinct terms exactly what you believe to be the purpose of this particular exercise and its relevance to film making or story-telling..

STEVE SANDERS

Um..well, um...I guess photographers learned ways of looking and seeing and recording people and the world from Artists; and then moving pictures developed from that. So logically looking at paintings old and new expands our understanding of light, focus, and colour and perspective that informs succinct storytelling through visual story telling in which words and dialogue can have added weight.. I'm not sure, it just seems like it happened that way?

DORIAN's grunts grudging approval.

DORIAN

Hmmm. Not a bad summary young SANDERS.

SANDERS' peers look at him somewhat differently. STEPHANIE winks at him and this really annoys a jealous JULIE.

Allons y tous le monde

JUSTIN and BERNADETTE grin at each other over DORIAN'S pretentious usage of FRENCH.

DORIAN

Let's not waste another minute.

He sets off at pace and the group hurry after him.

INT.STATE ART GALLERIES.DAY
A MONTAGE SCENE of the group as the group follow him around like a gaggle of TOURISTS trying to see the LOUVRE in twenty minutes. The STUDENTS are seen humorously Pixillated following in the "GREAT MAN man's" wake. From varying POVS they race from painting to painting and he gestures at each and spouts inaudible INFO with manic hand gestures. "BLIND" JULIE stands in front of a painting and acts as if it is rubbish. Several STUDENTS act out little theatre sport vignettes behind his back. JULIE turns her head every which way as she studies some paintings and even looks at it backwards through her legs. DORIAN stops in front of a huge and impressive portrait painting of an old LABOURER. He rubs his chin pretentiously for a moment and turns around to face them

DORIAN

I consider this to be the oeuvre of a middle order talent..

JULIE makes a puking face at the other STUDENTS.

More precisely, it's a piece of populist artistic pabulum - Baby food to you. Perfectly acceptable if created as revanchist snipe at the microcephalic vox populi of the mass media but otherwise, any comments mes camerades. Worse still, it is contrived and derivative and the story it tells is hollow and shrill. You there: Action Man..

WALLY

I'm sorry DORIAN but I don't understand some of the words you use. What's the bejesus does revanchist mean? Am I the only dope here who needs a dictionary when you talk

DORIAN (CHASTENED)

It means erm ..seeking to recover lost territory..

WALLY'S' face says "why didn't you say that then". DORIAN misses a step and finds another target.

>JUSTIN isn't it...? What is your considered response to this ... thing? And justify your answer.

JULIE'S still smirking as she whispers to BUI HUONG.

JULIE (A LITTLE TOO LOUDLY)

Intellectual TOSSERS always revert to a few throwaway esoteric phrases in a foreign language whenever they've got nothing CLEVER to say in their own language.

BUI HUONG's puzzled at Julie's turn of phrase and she consults her ubiquitous dictionary unsuccessfully.

JUSTIN:(UNCERTAINLY)

This is the first time I've seen this. I won't lie to you. Erm, I actually like it. To (CONT) me it seems to be original. And... it's true to life, I think.

DORIAN

Rubbish! It's all about discernment. Embrace acuity, nurture it....pursue
good taste"..which is welded to artistic perception and judgement.

JULIE (REMOVING GLASSES)

Surely "TASTE" in Painting or any ART form is culturally subjective and mired in intellectual snobbery though, DORIAN! What's so wrong with

JULIE (CONT)

the old adage about responding honestly to what you like. Spouting glib, European phrases and fancy words is all very well but who can prove beyond doubt it isn't a good painting? And I don't really understand how this picture is relevant to film making anyway.

DORIAN's face is suddenly drained of blood. He's clearly never been spoken to like this by a student. He visibly fights to control his temper and the other students look on in apprehensively.

DORIAN

When I want your opinion MS SLOANE, I'll tell you what it is. You're on thin ice her GIRLIE, so I suggest you join the others and bite your sharp tongue for a while.

SCENE.A LANDSCAPE AND PORTRAIT GALLERY.DAY. PIXILLATED
MONTAGE: The little group scurries from one work to the next. JULIE, BUI HUONG and JUSTIN make up the rear and do a little "OFF TO SEE THE WIZARD" style skipping behind DORIAN as he strides along, much to the amusement of the other STUDENTS. From the POV of one of the SECURITY GUARDS, JULIE goose-steps and makes the occasional HITLER moustache with her flattened finger under her nose. It's dangerous behaviour. WALLY looks sorry for DORIAN and makes a face at JULIE to cut it out.

INT PORTRAIT GALLERY SECTION.DAY
DORIAN has walked ahead and turns to see the GORUP has paused to look at two interesting FEMALE portraits, one of which is a physically challenged and miserable and destitute woman and the other a study in idealized FEMALE beauty and substance.

DORIAN: (IMPERIOUS)

Yes….tough choice indeed, comparing a beautiful and cosmopolitan E ENCHANTRESS with an ugly little HARRIDEN, SLATTERN, HOYDEN, TERMAGENT or common SHREW

JULIE:

So which do you prefer DORIAN?

PAN TO
The other STUDENTS are shocked by her rudeness. DORIAN'S incapable of speech for a moment. He flics his head at her and stomps the 10 metres to the divan with JULIE in his wake.. The OTHERS are silently staring as the drama unfolds.

DORIAN

How dare you speak to me like that in front of my STUDENTS you jumped up little bit…. Your FATHER might be the Executive Head but I'm not taking this from you or anyone else. What exactly is your bloody problem?

She realizes she's gone too far this time and verges on panic.

JULIE (GENUINE CONTRITION)

I'm very sorry DORIAN. I Didn't mean to be rude. It's very hard for me at FILM SCHOOL with my DAD. Everyone thinks he cheated for me to get the scholarship.

DORIAN fails to hide the fact he's one who thought that way.

JULIE

And also…

DORIAN

You might as well let me have it with the other barrel seeing you've gone this far..He's actually got a decent human side.

JULIE

Moreover..I thought you were totally unfair to me at that audition for your new films, as I know I did much better than you said I did and..He raises a hand, recognizing there's truth in her words.

DORIAN

Alright JULIE. You've spoken honestly and I hear what you are saying. I know I'm not the best of communicators at times.. but There are probably actually some worthwhile things I can teach you.

She nods in appreciation her his tolerance.

How about we shake hands and start over. Both try a bit harder. Deal?

She smiles and nods and they shake hands. DORIAN'S face shows he's learned a valuable lesson. From JULIE'S POV the rest of the class seem mightily relieved.

BUSHRANGER FESTIVAL VENUE. CLASSIC OLD MELBOURNE THEATRE .DAY.
It's opening night: a social affair of schmoozing with glitterati. MIKEstands with GONERIL and MERRIMAN

MIKE

Okay, you two cool cats have lapped up some decent champers, so given the level of crazy things about this virtual nut LEVEL industry you're so keen to

MIKE (CONT)

enter, indulge me on how you've learnt to distinguish between friend and foe..on the financing of films for instance?Believe a fifth of what you're told and always be vigilant. You used to be able to tell who was who to some extent by the suits – 't'was ONCE far easier to tell harmless reef sharks from tiger sharks who'd eat their own families, and spot guppies in shark skin suits .. identification skills count, but now the sharks and the sundry creative cats involved - excuse the mixed creature metaphors - are likelier to dress alike and look alike, but remember the time honoured maxim in movies, if an offer sounds too good to be true it invariably will be....so to set my mind at rest, PLEASE identify that fat cat over there.

He nods at a portly fiftyish man with bad posture, wearing tweed jacket with elbow patches, jeans and sneakers. The man has a mouthful of canapes and a glass of champagne in each hand he's quaffing and a festival program protruding from his pocket.

MERRIMAN

Um, I bet my life savings on his being a writer

MIKE (CHUCKLING)

Bingo! And that tomcat over there?

He flicks a glance at a well-built narcissistic late 30's male standing near the door and trying to make an entrance.

GONERIL

That would be an actor who's always yabbering on about his "craft"...and spends more than a tad too long looking in the mirror. Maybe he's also a stray cat between agents.

MIKE grins and nods.

MIKE

Svelte female at 2 o'clock.

A stylish but heavily intoxicated mid-twenties platinum blonde in a red dress and heels sashays awkwardly as she makes her way into the theatre

GONERIL

Alley-cat-atonic actress.

MICK

And what about that black cat over there.

He glances at a forty year old male with silver hair and dressed totally in black as he holds forth to a trio of attractive slightly older women.

MERRIMAN

No problem – plutocrat-mreaucatinvestor!

MIKE nods approval at both their assessments. He then spreads his arms indicating the whole room and as individuals of every shape and appearance pass by MERRIMAN assesses stereotypes and adds a few humorous assessments. Many are all in black

MERRIMAN(INDICATING PEOPLE WITH NODS)

Producer, Director, Executive Producer, Lawyer, actor, actor, writer, actor, call girl..um undertaker,... tinker.

MIKE

Gadzooks. Methinks thou and thou artready! Well the first of you and your peers' films will be screening in a few minutes. Confident?

The couple look at each other and shrug.

INT. VICTORIAN ERA THEATRES BUILDING.DUSK
The crowd exits from one theatre and MIKE and his two students are joined by the rest of their number and merge with another crowd as they head for the theatre entrance.

INT.THEATRE.DAY/NIGHT
WENDY AND JENN cross one of the aisles to sit with MIKE. They all look contented. After the lights go out the images move between their faces and moments from several short STUDENT films including ASTRAL BOY.

EXT.INT. UPMARKET BAR NEAR THE THEATRE.DAY
After the screening GONERIL, MERRIMAN and WALLY enter a nearby bar. MERRIMAN brings drinks and sees SLOANE in deep conversation with EASTER in a quiet booth not far away and becomes suspicious.

MERRIMAN

Well call me SUSPICIOUS SAM, but SLIPPERY SLOANE is sitting in a booth (CONT) over there chewing the fat with that dodgy film reviewer.

WALLY

EASTER?

MERRIMAN nods and they lean forward out of their booth trying to see them but they're tucked inside the deep booth in earnest talk. GONERIL and WALLY look at MERRIMN as if they expect him to do something. He looks in his satchel and removes a couple of electronic bugs and surreptitiously makes his way to the booth in question. When he gets close he pretends to do up his shoe and plant one of the bugs on a large pot plant obscuring the booth, and returns to his seat. Upon his return he puts on some small head phones to eavesdrop.

WALLY

You're a dangerous man THOMAS MERRIMAN.

INT.HOTEL BOOTH.
In their booth SLOANE and EASTER are quaffing wine and talkingconspiratorially, in low voices.

EASTER

This is an extremely serious decision BRYCE. I was able to justify my hatchet job article all those years ago…but this is, well, risky. If anyone found out.. well you can imagine the consequences for both of us I'm sure.

SLOANE

I'll definitely make it worth your while. How would anyone know they're all anonymous entries anyway, right? So no bias is possible. You only need to know the name of the "correct" title and it's a done deal.

EASTER's looks show acquiescence and sudden devious grin tells Sloane he'll do the deed and that it's now just a matter of price.

INT.HOTEL.DAY
In the other booth MERRIMAN passes the head phones to GONERIL and Wally and they share one each. GONERIL now shows some initiative and heads for the women's toilet and takes several telling photos of the conspirators in deep conversation with her smart phone.

INT.UPMARKET HOTEL.DAY

SLOANE

How does five score sound to you?

EASTER

A hundred thousand $Buckaroos? Well it's 's definitely in the ball park, I can tell you that. So Merci beaucoup mon ami. This meeting is hereby closed.

They shake hands and it's a done deal.. Easter accepts a wad of notes and watches Sloane head to the bar, to order something from the waitress and pay her before exiting the hotel. A few moments later the waitress approaches Sloane with a bottle of French champagne.

INT.UPMARKET HOTEL.DAY

GONERIL

Well those two are certainly up to no good. I've a feeling our friend, ISHMAEL, may be the intended victim here.

WALLY

Uh huh, it's MIKE alright. They had to be talking about that Open Screenplay competition at the BUSHRANGER FEST didn't they?

The other two nod in agreement.

GONERIL

It might be time we all exited this place before we're spotted.

They're with her on this and they exit furtively one by one

EXT. HOTEL WALKWAY NEAR THEATRES.NIGHT
The three of them wander through the Entertainment precinct.

GONERIL

So how do we play this you guys. SLOANE'S Head of School and could fail us instantly and kick us out. The Festival ends in two days and the winning script will be announced as the last event.

She shrugs helplessly.

MERRIMAN

If he's cheated, as we know he has, he should lose his job. Maybe MIKE's script wouldn't win anyway, but if it isn't given the same chance as all the others, itbrings the ACADEMY into disrepute; and it tarnishes our Academic results. It could damn our futures as well.

They all sit despondently on a bench on the tree lined boulevard.

WALLY

Between a rock and a hard place we are, as YODA might put it.

MERRIMAN

Or SCYLLA and CHARYBIDUS or the Devil and the deep blue..

GONERIL's comic glare shuts him up instantly. She's clearly curing him of his verbal affliction gradually.

WALLY

We need someone expert to help us, from someone unknown to them! Someone like, erm, like..

Suddenly MINH drops out of a nearby tree with a thud, like a NINJA

>   **MINH**
>
> Someone like MINH! I am Minder to BUI HUONG but MINH now work for other people also. Will help young FOOLISH wine drink Film STUDENTS fix problem with SLIPPERY! Okay?

The now wide eyed three take a reality check and listen to his plan enthusiastically.

INT.THEATRE BISTRO.NIGHT
JENN's's having a meal with WENDY

>   **WENDY**
>
> Mum, this is going to sound a bit suss because there's an older guy I seem drawn to.. erm..you know him too..

J
ENN looks suddenly apprehensive and stops eating.

>   **JENN**
>
> Oh please don't tell me you're talking about MIKE! Just Don't say you've dated ...Him!

>   **WENDY**
>
> Plenty of women date older MEN; but no, not so far.

>   **JENN**
>
> Thank God for that!

JENN takes an old diary from her leather bag and removes a few photos from inside the book. She hands over two photogenic pictures of herself and MIKE aged in their early twenties and romantically entwined. WENDY's eyes widen.

JENN

Like most people I've done a few things in my life I'm not proud of, but this one is actually shameful. I was young when I got pregnant with you. I was young and vulnerable and emotionally not too bright. And I was angry with him.

Wendy is looking increasingly uncomfortable. Jenn doesn't know how to continue.

JENN

MIKE was erm, a difficult young man back then. BRYCE, MICK and even DORIAN all, wanted me, I suppose is the correct term. Though I think DORIAN. They were all high maintenance, though. I had no interest in DORIAN, except as a friend. And..not much interest in.....

WENDY is now really uncomfortable

I don't know how to begin to tell you Sweetheart. I beg your forgiveness but.. JESUS! BRYCE is not your biological father, LOVE..WENDY's stunned, bereft.

She stands so abruptly her Chair falls over.

WENDY

You can't. mean...my real father is? But I could have had a proper Father all these years and…that is unforgivable!

JENN tearfully stands and walks towards her but WENDY turns and storms out looking bereft, as well as furious.

EXT. CITY NIGHT CLUB.NIGHT
It's late when SLOANE exits an upmarket nightclub arm in arm with BUI HUONG. They're tipsy and amorous as they walk along the increasingly deserted street. Suddenly a man materializes behind them dressed in black, his face hidden by a scarf.

> **MINH**
>
> I have Luger hand gun pointed at both you. Please to walk off street into lane over there.
>
> **SLOANE (STARTING TO TURN ROUND)**
>
> Listen BUDDY, if it's money you want..I've only got $400 in cash but it's yours.
>
> **MINH**
>
> Both to face front. Not want money.

Bui Huong is whimpering in fear and Sloane is terrified as well.

> **MINH (NOW IN VIETNAMESE)**
>
> BUI HUONG I was sent here by your father to look after you.

She's shocked and snatches a glance at him over her shoes

> You have not behaved as your mother and father wished, but I too have learned how seductive this country can be, so… But this man you with is a bad man. Leave now and not look back. He will give you good role in film soon MINH promise. But you must no further romance with him. This is not what say you, negotiable, or MINH arrange for you return HANOI. Understood BUI HUONG?

She nods hard and leaves without turning round. He then pushes SLOANE further down the alleyway and changes to his broken English.

SLOANE

Please don't hurt me. I can get you more money within an hour. Please..

MINH

No money. You bad man romance young Vietnamese woman. Your student. Other bad thing IS you cheat teacher O'LEARY. MINH know you pay EASTER BAD EGGin BUSHRANGER FESTIVAL screenplay competition. Have witnesses. You have one chance now - do what I say and change who SLOANE is. Change Sloane for better. Understand.

SLOANE

Who the fuck are you?

MINH

MINH is Person Australian people say that ONRY FRUCKWITS mess with! Please to answer MINH question. You
change SLOANE or you lose job, lose reputation, lose friends, lose family. Lose all things important!

SLOANE

Yes! Yes. I agree. I do. I truly do! Really..He can stand it no longer and turns around, but MINH has disappeared.

INT.CASINO HIGH ROLLERS ROOM.NIGHT
Percy arrives to gamble and drink to excess. From a distance he sees a hive of activity at one of the tables and he sees and curvy blonde in a slinky black dress with her back to him who seems to winning big time. He Grabs a glass of wine from a waiter and wanders over. Peering through the craning onlookers he admires the attractive

woman winning and then does a double take. His eyes bulge as he realizes it's his wife looking like a knockout. She glances up at him from across the table for a moment and smiles, waves and gives him a sultry look. She is the epitome of the beautiful girls Percy seems to be interested in and he's smitten.

AGNES KELLY-SLATER

Hello PERCY. I'm on a streak. Care to join me Handsome?

FILM FESTIVAL THEATRES.NIGHT

It's the finale to the festival and Prize giving night. Everyone who's anyone in the industry is there, All are in high spirits and enthusiastically applaud the winners. MIKE's students are announced as second place getters in the major category of best short film of WALLY'S "EUCALYPTO BLACK". SLOANE looks marginally-comatose and possibly shocked.. For the Final major prize for best original screenplay winner is announced by a sheepish EASTER.

EASTER (INGRATIATING)

Well, I have to admit this festival has been a rip-roaring success and the standard of work is of immense credit to all entrants and especially to the winners. It is now my privilege to announce the winner for best Original Screenplay WITH the production fillip of $3.000.000 is local film maker and lecturer...MIKE O'Leary.

The applause is very enthusiastic as MIKE stands unsteadily and walks to the stage disbelievingly as he accepts a statuette and a cheque..

MIKE

I have to say I'm speechless! Well not quite but I mean I don't have a speech. It's been a great honour

MIKE (CONT)

> teaching such a fine group of young film makers this year and they've given me something I lost a long time ago - a belief in the craft and in myself. So I really owe these 12 students

He gestures to the students who are sitting in a row close

> I owe them big time as they have taught me a lot more than I taught them and I know they are all destined to make their mark in the industry and their second place in the thriller section proves that.

He is now lost for words and MERRIMAN and then the rest of his class and the entire audience stand and applaud loudly. JENN is tearful and waves at WENDY, who ignores her.

AFTER PARTY AT NEARBY NIGHT CLUB RESTAURANT.NIGHT

TINSEL AND LIGHTS decorations and a huge brightly lit Christmas tree are a backdrop to the celebrations. Everyone is there and toasting MIKE. WENDY approaches him and gives him a big loving hug which confuses him for a moment. He gives her a puzzled look as JENN too hugs him. He watches as the two WOMEN slowly approach each other. Forgiveness happens and they are a family once more. BERNADETTE now steps up onto the low stage where a band is tuning their instruments. She raises a full glass of champagne for a toast.

BERNADETTE

> Well I think I speak for all of us when I say we're all ready for a MERRY CHRISTMAS and

BERNADETTE (CONT)

a long holiday and this year couldn't have finished on a better note. So I'd like you all to raise your glasses and drink a toast to our inspiring teachers this year, JENN and DORIAN and BRYCE...and MIKE.
And contrary to what you think, MIKE we all now agree you are no longer the grumpy old FART who started us off on the journey we took so far this year: I think you have rediscovered your writing and directing Mojo and we all believe next year you will achieve some of the success you so richly deserved for your first feature film all those years ago.

He's humbled and they all drink a toast.

And one more thing: JUSTIN and I are having a baby! AND we're getting married!

They're all pretty stunned but very happy for them both and cheer loudly. GONERIL, merry with Gluwein grabs the microphone now.

GONERIL (FOUR POINTS TO THE WIND)

Well done JUSTIN ! I didn't think you had it in you. And now it's been in BERNADETTE as well.

She's weird but good. They're smile, finally friends.

So if I have everyone's permission, I'd like to say in the now-immortal words of CHARLES DICKENS' character GRIMEYBLING, in A CHRISTMAS CAROL, God Bless us every one.

They all raise their glasses again and JENN and WENDY and all the students and DORIAN raise their glasses to the expecting couple and then to MIKE, who now KNOWS all his Christmases have come at once.
BILLY's ghost appears for a few seconds and shows his acceptance of his circumstances and satisfaction with his brother's success and contentment.

THE END

www.ingramcontent.com/pod-product-compliance
Lightning Source LLC
Chambersburg PA
CBHW060609080526
44585CB00013B/754